To Kennedy,
Don't be afraid to Shine
V. Bartles
29 Apr 2017

Twelve Steps

VERONICA BARTLES

TWELVE STEPS is a work of fiction. Names, characters, places, and incidents are either products of the author's imagination or are used fictitiously. Any resemblance to actual persons, living or dead, business establishments, events, or locales is entirely coincidental.

Copyright © 2014 by Veronica Bartles.
Second Edition

TWELVE STEPS by Veronica Bartles All rights reserved. Published in the United States of America by Kissing Frogs Press. First published in the United States of America by Swoon Romance.

No part of this book may be used or reproduced in any manner whatsoever without written permission of the author, except in the case of brief quotations embodied in critical articles and reviews.

ISBN: 978-0692636725
ISBN: 0692636722

Edited by Mandy Schoen
Cover design by VBartles Design
Cover copyright © 2015 by Veronica Bartles
Cover license via Dollar Photo Club

This book is dedicated to:

Amy, "the future first female President of the United States" (you have my vote!),

Jason, who told me I could do anything I set my mind to,

and

Monica, who believed in me enough to keep a slip of paper with my autograph for 22 years, while waiting for this day to arrive.

Way back in junior high school, you made me promise to dedicate my first book to you. Your faith in me kept me going, even when I couldn't muster faith in myself. Now, I'm thrilled to be able to keep my promise.
Love you guys!!

Chapter One

There should be a support group for kids with perfect siblings. Something like AlaTeen, but without the drug talk. We could sit around and chat about how our flawless family members are systematically destroying our lives.

"Hello, my name is Andrea Andersen, and I am a second-class sibling." And if my sister weren't so freakishly perfect, I wouldn't still be grounded.

I grab the last handful of hangers out of my closet and hurl the clothes onto the growing pile on my bed. It's not like one little D in biology would have ruined my life. My A-plus in history should have balanced it out.

After more than a week of serious butt kissing, I almost convinced Mom to ease up on my sentence, but then Laina piped up with "maybe if you stopped skipping class, you wouldn't be failing."

Well, maybe if Mr. Keeler didn't always compare me with Laina, I wouldn't need to ditch.

I throw my shoes, one by one, into the middle of my bedroom floor. I'm so not in the mood to sort through my clothes for Laina's annual clothing drive.

I ignore a sharp knock, but Mom opens my door anyway. "Jarod's here," she says. "You can talk for ten minutes."

I scramble to my feet, smoothing my clothes and yanking my hair into a loose bun.

Jarod never comes over for just me. Even when I used to help him run lines for the school play, he always made sure Laina would be around. I've always been an excuse for him to drool over the Princess of Perfection. Even though I was friends with Jarod first, my sister was the one he noticed.

But I've been grounded for nearly two weeks. Maybe he's missed me.

"Are you sure he wanted me?" I ask. "Not Laina?"

Mom sighs and looks at me like I'm stupid. "He said it was important. And your ten minutes start now." She pushes a button to start the stopwatch feature on her phone and stalks off toward her bedroom.

I scurry in the opposite direction, grateful for once that Mom plays favorites. She wouldn't give me even ten minutes for anyone other than Jarod.

Ironically, I might have had a real chance with him if it weren't for mom's lopsided angel food cake and Mrs. Johnson's extra crispy brownies at the *Much Ado About Nothing* cast reception.

Jarod and I were extras together in the community theater production, back in the summer before Jarod and Laina started junior high. We bonded over a mutual love of Shakespeare, and I was almost sure he liked me, too.

But then my sister decided to watch my rehearsals.

The minute Laina walked into the auditorium with her tight tops, short skirts and newly-sprouted boobs, Jarod totally forgot I was alive. He got so distracted watching her that the director had to give Jarod's one line to another actor.

When our mothers bonded over their failed desserts,

Mrs. Johnson mentioned Jarod's "little crush," and Mom flew into full-on matchmaker mode. She pushed Laina into Jarod's life every chance she could get, even convincing the Johnsons to start attending worship services with us on Sundays, "so the kids could get to know each other better."

Laina and Jarod have been practically joined at the hip ever since.

For the past six years, I've been nothing but Laina's freckled and awkward, metal-mouthed, frizzy-haired, little sister. And even though I ditched the braces last fall and I finally figured out how to use a straightening iron on my hair without frying the ends, I didn't think Jarod would ever see me as anything more than Laina's little sister.

But this time, he's here for me.

At the end of the hall, I stop to gather my composure and plan my approach. I pull a few strands of hair out of my bun to frame my face and check my reflection in the mirror hanging in the middle of some old family photos. Quickly flipping through a catalog of emotions, I decide my safest bet is to appear slightly bored, yet curious. Jarod would totally shut down if I came on too strong.

Mom only gave me ten minutes to work my magic. I can't blow this by getting all squealy and excited.

Thomas Jefferson once said, "Nothing gives a person so much advantage over another as to remain always cool and unruffled under all circumstances." And I need every advantage I can get.

I walk into the living room and manage not to trip over my own feet when Jarod smiles at me. "Hey," I say in my best casual voice. "What's up?"

Jarod takes a step toward me and looks over my shoulder. "Your mom isn't going to come in here, is she? This is kind of private." He's close enough that I can feel his warm breath on my cheek.

I shiver and shove my hands into my pockets, so he

won't see them shaking. It would be so easy to turn my head just a fraction of an inch and kiss him, but Jarod's kind of a traditionalist. I have to let him make the first move, or I risk scaring him off.

"No, I have at least eight more minutes before the warden sends me back to solitary confinement." I move to the couch and collapse onto the soft cushions. Hugging one of mom's giant throw pillows to my chest, I take a deep breath to slow my pulse and calm my quivering nerves.

His mouth curls up into a slow, sexy grin and I have to look away. I concentrate on separating the strands of fringe along the edge of the throw pillow as he crosses the room. Anything to distract myself.

Jarod stands over me and pulls on one of my loose curls. "Did I catch you in the middle of a nap?" he asks. "You look a little out of it." I'm suddenly ultra-conscious of my rumpled sweats. I wish I'd taken time to change into something sexier.

I ditch the pillow and resist the urge to fix my hair. I have to be cool and unruffled. "Nope. Just rockin' the can't-leave-the-house casual look today. And you're stalling." I pat the cushion beside me. "What do you need?"

Jarod perches on the opposite edge of the couch and clasps his hands in his lap. A second later, he stands up again. A slow blush creeps across his cheeks, and he wipes his palms on his jeans. He runs his fingers through his dark hair, and then he sits down, a few inches closer to me.

I wait while he picks at an imaginary speck of lint on the couch cushion between us. I've never seen him so nervous. Not even around Laina.

I lick my lips. I'm not going to kiss him first, but it doesn't hurt to be ready.

"I need you," he finally says, reaching out to take my hand and gazing into my eyes.

This is the point where I usually wake up. I pinch my

arm hard enough to leave an angry, red welt, but Jarod is still here, still smiling at me, still waiting for me to say something.

Oh, crap, he's waiting for me to say something.

I take a deep breath to calm the miniature acrobats practicing backflips in my stomach. But Jarod is tracing lazy circles on the back of my hand with his thumb, and there's no calming my bubbling insides. He leans closer, and the smell of his watermelon-mint gum mixed with the musky scent of his cologne is nearly enough to drive me over the edge.

I pull back a bit. Not enough so I'll seem uninterested, but enough that he'll have to put in some effort when he decides to go for it. "You do?" My casual voice is gone, replaced by a nervous squeak.

"I do." He smiles and releases my hand. "I've tried everything, but Laina still won't go out with me."

"Yeah," I say, leaning in to seal his confession with a kiss. I can't believe Jarod Johnson wants me. He needs me. He—Wait, what?

"Thanks, Andi. You're a great friend. I knew I could count on you to talk to her for me." He hugs me and then slumps against the back of the couch with a grin.

I want to slap that smile right off his face. To scream and cry and beg him to love me. But of course, I won't. This isn't some cheesy soap opera. Real life takes finesse. Now, more than ever, I have to remain unruffled and in control. Because Laina's had Jarod on a string for six years.

She's had her chance with him.

I yawn and peel myself off the couch, stretching slowly. "Yeah, well, if that's all you need, I guess I'd better get back to my room. I'm pretty sure my ten minutes are up." I saunter out of the room, careful not to let any kind of emotion show.

I totally need a twelve-step program.

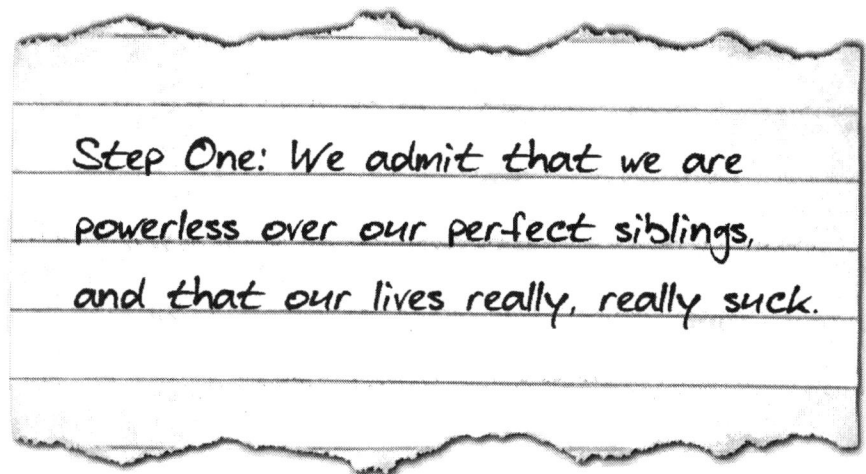

Chapter Two

When my best friend, Summer, started going to AlaTeen meetings last year, after her mom's drinking got out of control, she explained that acceptance is always the first step to fixing anything. You have to admit that you have a problem. Because no matter how much you try to ignore it, the issue will never, ever go away unless you have the courage to face it.

So, yeah, I admit it. My life completely sucks. All because of my super-brilliant, gorgeous, God's-gift-to-the-entire-universe, perfect older sister, Alaina.

It's not that I don't love her. I totally do. But Laina's ability to go through life without ever once making a single mistake makes the rest of us normal people look bad. And no mere mortal can compete with her awesomeness.

Laina took her first steps when she was six months old. She potty trained herself before her first birthday. And she was already reading by the time she turned three. Because she was their first child, my parents thought this behavior was completely normal. They thought I was "developmentally challenged" because I wasn't speaking in full sentences at ten months old. Laina sets the bar so high, it's impossible to reach.

If I tried, I could wrap my teachers around my little finger, like she does. High school teachers are the easiest people in the world to manipulate. All you have to do is pretend to think they're fascinating, and suddenly they think you're the best thing since sliced bread. But Laina's already been there, done that, and if the best part I can hope for is understudy, why bother trying out?

There's supposed to be a balance between sisters. One gets the brains, and the other gets the looks, but I didn't even get to be the "pretty one." Laina grabbed that title too, long before I had a chance to grow out of my awkward phase. To say Laina developed early would be a serious understatement. When all of her friends were still afraid to take the training wheels off their bikes, Laina was already trying on training bras. While I waited for braces and zit cream to work their magic on me, Laina grew into a real-life Barbie doll, complete with a whole flock of adoring Ken wannabes, following her around like so many little, lost puppies.

Last year, after our marching band totally failed in the State Finals, Laina decided that people didn't take her seriously enough. She suddenly started hiding under oversized t-shirts and baggy jeans, but I don't know what she thought that would accomplish. She said something about wanting people to notice her mind, not just her boobs, but you can't hide a mountain range under a drop cloth.

Now, the guys are more anxious than ever to try to peel away the layers and reveal the hot body underneath. Normal girls can't compete with looks like hers, and I never even got a real chance with Jarod before she snapped him up as part of her harem.

The only role Laina didn't claim was "cute and

carefree," because that label doesn't mesh well with sheer, unadulterated perfection. So I'm the fun one. The one who doesn't care what anyone thinks. The one who has no problem ditching third period to hang out at the park across the street with Nick Carver, because making out with him is better than listening to Mr. Keeler's boring biology lectures.

It isn't as easy as you'd think to keep up the act, but what other choice do I have? I can't exactly be nothing.

Laina strolls into my bedroom without bothering to knock. She tosses me an unopened package of Oreos, and then she shoves the piles of sorted clothes into a heap on the floor so she can flop onto my bed. "You skipped dinner. Thought you could use some sustenance." She runs her fingers through her long, blonde hair and examines it for split ends. Sometimes, I think it must be super exhausting to keep up her level of perfection.

"Thanks." I force a smile and slowly open the package of cookies.

"I don't know how you can eat all the junk you do. I would feel like such a slug if my diet was like yours."

"Yeah, well, thanks for not judging me or anything." I drop the cookies on my bedside table. She could have brought me carrot sticks or salad if she was so concerned about my eating habits, instead of bringing me cookies as a substitute for dinner.

I grab several hangers and shove them back into my closet before reaching for the rest. Laina already has everything else. She doesn't need my clothes for her precious clothing drive.

"Uh-oh," Laina says. "If Oreos can't fix whatever this is, it must be serious. What's up?"

"My sister's only ruining my life," I mutter. "No big deal."

"Well, isn't that what big sisters are for?" She bats her eyelashes and flashes a goofy grin.

She's obviously trying to make me smile, but I'm not exactly in a smiling mood. I glare at her and start tossing shoes back into the closet. But Laina amps up her grin and adds an exaggerated shoulder shimmy and hair flip. "I'm just doing my job."

I can't help laughing a little bit. "You're good at it."

"I'm sorry." She pauses and frowns. "Um, I don't actually know what I did wrong."

"You didn't do anything wrong. You never do."

I grab the Oreos and flop onto the bed beside her. I pop a whole cookie into my mouth and chew it slowly, buying time to gather my thoughts. It's not fair for me to be angry. Laina can't help being perfect and adorable.

And for someone so smart, she's totally clueless when it comes to anything real. I honestly don't think she realizes that half of the guys in school are totally in lust with her. She's never even noticed that her best friend is a jealous witch who spends every waking moment trying to convince Laina that she'll never be good enough. And she doesn't know she does the same thing to me. But the thing is, Laina's not trying to make me miserable. She's just so determined to make everything perfect that she never realizes how frustrating it is to have my every flaw analyzed.

"I really am sorry you're so upset. You can yell at me, if it helps," Laina says.

Of course I'm not going to yell at her. But obviously, I can't tell her about Jarod's visit this afternoon either. If she ever stopped being so clueless and realized he's in love with her, I'd lose any hope of a chance with him.

I swallow hard and sit up, crossing my legs and leaning against the headboard. "You should be sorry. You'd think a straight-A student like you would be smart enough to realize that Oreos cannot be properly devoured without the requisite glass of milk." I frown and stare at my empty hands, as if waiting for milk to magically appear.

"Oops!" Laina jumps up, giggling, and races out of the room.

I feel the slightest twinge of guilt over manipulating her compulsive need to please people, but sometimes Laina's neuroses totally come in handy. And right now, I really need a few minutes to plan my next move. Thomas Jefferson's advice about being cool and unruffled is perfect in almost every situation, but sometimes life requires a little bit of carefully-constructed drama. And if I'm going to get ungrounded in time to show Jarod he's going after the wrong sister, this is definitely one of those times.

Laina returns a few minutes later and hands me a tall glass of cold milk. I carefully twist open an Oreo and lick out the crème filling before dunking the cookie part into my milk.

"Okay, now will you tell me what's bothering you?" Laina asks.

I blink back a few well-timed tears. "Nothing. I'm fine. Really." I dissect another cookie.

"Come on. You can tell me."

I take a deep, shaky breath and set the cup and the decimated cookie on my nightstand. Then, I shrug and pick at imaginary balls of lint on my quilt.

Laina wraps an arm around me and pulls me in for a protective, big-sister hug. "Talk to me. Maybe I can help."

I shake my head and pull away. "I'm just so tired of being grounded. You'd think they could overlook one silly, little D. I still have a B average, and who cares about biology anyway?" I frown and look up at her through droopy eyelashes. "What's it like, being the favorite child?"

Laina laughs nervously. "Mom and Dad are just as hard on me as they are on you. More, even, since I'm the oldest."

I snort. "Really? So Mom didn't go storming into Ms. Detweiler's office to demand justice when you got a D last year? Because I don't remember you ever being grounded for a whole semester."

"Well, that was only because Ms. Shea hated me."

"Yeah. I love how my D means I'm a failure, but your D means you were being picked on. You're right." I sigh and sniffle, squeezing out another tear. "They don't have a favorite daughter at all."

Laina squirms. "Well, gym is different. I wasn't failing a real class like biology." Her voice trails off as I glare at her. "I'm sorry."

I exhale slowly and then take a long swallow of milk. Time to move in for the kill. "No. I'm sorry. I shouldn't complain." I put on my best trying-to-be-brave-but-not-quite-succeeding face and smile weakly, dabbing at my eyes with the edge of my sleeve. "It's just ..."

Laina leans toward me, layers of concern etched into her expression. She's fully in protective-big-sister mode now, and all I have to do is plant a few seeds.

"I didn't even get to go to the Snow Ball last weekend," I complain. "It was your big night, and I wasn't even there to watch you be crowned Snow Queen." I squeeze my eyes shut to prevent a flood of real tears. I had been so certain that I'd be elected Snow Queen, but I wasn't even nominated. Meanwhile, Laina didn't want to go to the ball, and she didn't campaign, but she still won by a landslide. Because it's not enough for her to get everything she wants. She has to get everything I want, too.

"It's really not that big of a deal," she says. "It was just a stupid dance."

I dissect another cookie, trying to regain my control. "I'm missing everything important. And it's not like me being cooped up in my bedroom has made Mr. Keeler any less boring. It's not going to improve my grade."

"Do you want me to talk to Mom for you?"

I shake my head and push the corners of my mouth up into an obviously fake smile. She'll be more persuasive if she can honestly tell Mom that I didn't ask her to intervene. "No. I'm okay. I'm just a little whiny today. But the pity party's over. I promise."

"Well, if you need anything, let me know, okay?" Laina hugs me again and I nod. She stands up and stretches. "I have a ton of homework to do, but we'll talk later, okay?"

She strolls out of the room, pausing to look back at me when she reaches the door. I ignore the twinge of guilt that seizes my chest and wipe away a genuine tear rolling down my cheek. I wouldn't be manipulating Laina if I had any other options. But Mom and Dad never say no to their favorite daughter, and I'm desperate.

By tomorrow morning, I'll be free, and then I can show Jarod what he's missing.

Chapter Three

"You got your parents to drop the grounding?" Emily asks. "How did you pull that off?" She slides her lunch tray onto the table and rips open a packet of ketchup. After carefully squeezing squiggly red lines over her pile of limp cafeteria fries, Emily looks at me expectantly, as if I hold the answer to all of life's secrets.

Summer rolls her eyes and takes a swig of her Diet Coke. "Andi's a total kiss-up, didn't you know?"

"I cleaned the garage," I say. "Mom's been bugging Dad to do it for months, and he was never going to get around to it. Everyone has a price. Even parents."

Emily laughs. "You really are the master manipulator, aren't you? Have you ever not gotten out of a punishment?"

"Yeah, well, I don't really believe in paying for my mistakes. That's boring." Laina's face flashes in my mind, and I swallow a flutter of remorse as I think about the way I used her. But if Laina hadn't set such impossible standards, Mom and Dad wouldn't have had a fit over my biology grade in the first place. And if she'd kept her big mouth shut, I could have talked my way out of the grounding on my own. It was only fair that Laina should negotiate my release. I should be commended for my resourcefulness.

I have nothing to feel guilty about.

I flip my hair over my shoulder and grin as Emily nods thoughtfully.

Summer shakes her head. "You are my hero."

It doesn't matter that I'm obviously lying through my teeth. They believe me, because they want to.

My eyes flit across the cafeteria to where Jarod is sitting with his friends, Josh and Rob, and I turn the sigh that escapes my lips into an I'm-so-bored-with-this-topic exhalation. Admitting that I sometimes fail to get what I want goes against the whole persona I've worked so hard to construct.

Dave Maestas stops next to our table, balancing his lunch tray in one hand and a stack of books in the other, and totally blocks my view. "Hi Andi," he says, subtly shifting position every time I try to look around him, so that I'm forced to acknowledge his presence. "Have you picked a research topic for Mr. Mayer's class yet?"

"Of course." History is the one class worthy of my time, and Mr. Mayer makes it totally fun with these crazy research projects instead of exams. I've had all of my topics picked since the second week of school. I take a giant bite of my cheeseburger, hoping Dave will get the hint and go away.

Instead, he sets his lunch on the table beside me and pushes his fingers through his wavy, brown hair, causing it to stick up at odd angles. "I was thinking, maybe we could partner on this one. You're the only one in class who's even close to my level, and I really don't want to get stuck with someone who won't pull his weight again."

I nearly choke on my cheeseburger. "Are you implying that you have a higher grade than me in Mayer's class? I kicked your butt on that last project."

Dave grins, his brown eyes sparkling mischievously. "So you're paying attention to my grades now, huh? What do you say, partner, want to get together after school to plan our strategy?" He grabs his lunch tray and balances it on top of his books before tossing a fry into his mouth.

I roll my eyes. "I told you, I already have a plan. You'll have to find some other sucker to do your work for you."

He shrugs and walks away. "Maybe next time."

I shudder and Summer laughs. "Come on, Andi. He's not that bad." She turns around to watch him walk across the cafeteria. "I think he's kind of cute."

"You can have him." I frown as Dave drops his books onto an empty table between me and Jarod. If I didn't know better, I'd think he planned it. I can't even sneak a peek at Jarod without looking right past Dave.

Emily throws a fry at me, and I duck out of the way, narrowly avoiding an unsightly ketchup stain.

"You aren't even listening to us, are you? I could be confessing to a gory, violent crime, or professing my undying love for you here, and you wouldn't even notice," she says.

"Sorry, I was thinking. And I already know you want my body, so that's not exactly a huge revelation, Em." I raise my eyebrows and she laughs. "So now that I'm forgiven, tell me what I missed when I was so rudely ignoring my utterly fascinating best friends." I reach across the table, snag the rest of her uneaten fries and pop them into my mouth, all at once, before she can lob any more ketchup bombs at my head.

"See?" Emily says to Summer, waving her hand at me, like she's one of those game show girls showing off the big prizes. "This is why I hate her." She turns to me with an exaggerated frown. "How can you eat all that junk and stay so pencil thin? I have to count every single calorie, and work out for, like, an hour every day just so I don't look like a total cow."

"Whatever, Em," I say. "You're adorable." She's obviously forgotten about when I was a chubby, frizzy, freckled mess back in junior high, and I'm not about to remind her.

I work too hard to make beauty look effortless.

"And you could never look like a cow," Summer says. "You don't have the udders for it." She shimmies, and then she glances over her shoulder and winks at the group of freshman boys watching her from the next table. They duck their heads and start shoveling food into their mouths.

Emily laughs. "Whatever. I don't expect pretty people like you and Andi to understand my pain. You wouldn't know what to do with yourselves if you didn't have your little fan clubs following you around the school."

"I could set you up with someone," I say.

Emily huffs and folds her arms across her chest. "I don't want your leftovers." She shakes her head in disgust. "What's it like to be every guy's fantasy girl?"

I snort. "Yeah, that's me. I'm a sailor's dream. Sunken chest and all." I wave my hand across my front to indicate my barely-there B-cups. "At least you have some curves."

Summer giggles. "Whatever, Andi. Your boobs are fine. I haven't seen any guys complaining. Not every boy is obsessed with giant boobs, you know. Only the real creeps."

She glances to the overcrowded table in the center of the cafeteria, where Laina and her best friend, Kendra, sit surrounded by the entire varsity football team. Laina laughs at whatever asinine thing the quarterback says, and then she yawns and stretches, capturing the attention of every male within a fifty-foot radius in one fell swoop.

Except Dave.

He's staring at me like some creepy stalker guy, and when I glance over to see if Jarod is participating in the ogle-fest, Dave waves at me and winks. As if we're sharing some kind of private joke. He smiles slowly, revealing a dimple in his left cheek, and I have to remind myself not to smile back. He's much too cocky as it is.

"Yeah, I wouldn't want to date a creep." I roll my eyes at Dave and then turn my attention back to my friends. "So what movie are we going to see tomorrow?"

"I don't know," Summer says. "Maybe that one about the race car driver who robs a bank?"

Emily giggles. "Yeah, Summer wants an excuse to hang out with Josh again. She heard him and Rob talking about it in first period."

Summer blushes. "I know. I'm pathetic. But we had so much fun at the Snow Ball, and he's called me three times since, but he hasn't officially asked me out again. So, yeah."

I glance across the cafeteria as the bell rings. "You're not being pathetic. Let's do it." If Josh and Rob are going to the movie this weekend, Jarod will be there, too.

The scent of buttered popcorn fills the air, and my mouth waters as I step into line with Summer and Emily to buy our tickets for *Fiero Furious*. I don't see Jarod or his friends, but the movie starts in ten minutes. They're probably already inside.

"Hey, Andi. What's up?" Dave appears in line behind me.

"Are you following me now?" I take a half-step away from him, carefully maneuvering so that Emily stands as a buffer between us.

He laughs and points to the long line forming behind him. "I guess, if getting in line behind you means I'm following you, then I'm guilty as charged. But so are about thirty other people."

I cross my arms and turn my back on him. "Whatever. I

just think it's awfully coincidental that you happen to show up right after we get in line."

"You're right. I planned it. Because it's completely unbelievable that two random people could both want to go to the movies. On a Friday night. At the only good theater in town."

"Hey, Dave, what's up?" Summer asks, giving me her patented, exaggerated eye roll. I can practically hear her thoughts screaming at me. *What are you so afraid of? Dave's harmless. It's not like he's going to attack you right here in the middle of the mall.* But she wasn't there when Dave tried to kiss me in the coat closet after recess in fourth grade. She'd be freaked out too if some guy had been flirting with her nonstop since they were nine years old, even though she kept telling him she wasn't interested.

Dave is totally following me. I'd bet anything that he was listening to our conversation in the cafeteria. I bet he doesn't even like race car movies, and he's only here because he wanted a chance to "accidentally" run into me. And if Summer can't see what a creepy stalker he is, I'll just have to prove it.

I give Dave a million-megawatt smile. "What movie are you going to see?"

He blushes and points to a little boy who's probably about four years old hiding behind his leg. "My aunt and uncle are visiting, and I promised my cousin I'd take him to see *Ninja Unicorn Strikes Back*. He's a little shy, so my aunt always worries that he isn't socialized enough. Not sure that hanging out with his old cousin counts, but he's a cool kid, so it's all good. What are you here for?"

Very clever. Of course he'd choose a different movie, so he could pretend to be all innocent. And I have to give him bonus points for bringing along a decoy kid. I bend down and wave at the cute, little mini-Dave. "You like ninja unicorns?"

The little boy nods solemnly and releases his death grip

on Dave's pant leg.

I glance at Dave and then smile at the kid. "How long did Dave make you wait around for us to show up before you got into line?" That's one thing Dave didn't count on. Kids always tell the truth. He is so busted.

The little boy smiles and pats my cheek. "You have lots and lots of freckles," he says.

I stand up quickly and cover my face with my hands. Summer and Emily are laughing so hard they're practically rolling on the floor. "Well, it was nice meeting you," I say and shuffle forward as the line slowly advances, leaving my friends to fend for themselves.

Dave scoops the demon kid up and closes the gap between us. "We think your freckles are adorable." He hugs the kid. "Don't we?"

The little boy nods. "I like freckles."

I shrug and try to look unruffled, but I'm pretty sure my burning cheeks have blown my cover. I move up in line again and glare at the guy in the ticket booth. How long does it take to collect money and print tickets anyway?

"Yeah, so I guess you're here to see that?" Dave closes the gap between us and points over my shoulder to the poster for *Paris Romance* hanging on the wall next to the ticket booth.

"Nope. I saw that last weekend. And it was really good, so you can wipe that judgmental smile right off your face." I pass my money through the little window and collect my ticket.

"*Fiero Furious*? Really?" Dave asks, pulling the ticket out of my hand and inspecting it, as if he's sure he heard wrong. "I didn't think that was your type of movie."

"I guess you don't know me as well as you thought you did." I grab the ticket and shove it into my pocket. "I love movies like this."

"Oh, really?" Dave sets his cousin down and folds his arms. "Well, I'd love to talk to you afterward and hear your thoughts about the race scene and how it compares with *Silver Blaze*."

I shrug. "I don't know. Most sequels aren't as good as the originals, so I don't have high expectations. *Blaze* will be tough to beat. But I've seen good reviews for this one anyway. It's a totally different plotline this time around."

Dave laughs. "It's definitely a different plotline. Especially since *Silver Blaze* is a Sherlock Holmes short story and has nothing to do with race cars or bank robbers. But I'm sure you already knew that."

I can't believe I fell for that.

Dave just gets me so flustered, and I can't think clearly when he starts spouting off about things. He always acts like he knows me so well, but if he really knew me at all, he'd know I hate being made fun of. I walk away without answering. I don't have to prove anything.

"Bye!" Dave's cousin yells.

I turn around and smile at him. "Have fun with your ninjacorns and keep your cousin out of trouble," I say.

The boy smiles and squeezes Dave's hand. "I like her," I hear him whisper. "She's really pretty."

I push through the doors and into the theater lobby, and Summer runs right into me when I stop dead in my tracks.

"What's wrong with you? Why are you stopping?" she asks.

Jarod and his friends are standing in line, waiting to buy popcorn, and Laina is right in the middle of the group, basking in their undivided attention.

"Laina hates action movies," I say.

"Then what's she doing here?" Emily asks.

Summer frowns as Josh laughs at something Laina says, and I cringe when Jarod puts his arm around her shoulder to lead her away from the concession stand. By the time we get in line to buy popcorn, Jarod and his friends have followed Laina into the theater for *Ninja Unicorn*.

"Great," I mutter. "We wasted our money on a movie none of us wants to watch, and the guys didn't even see us."

I grab my snacks from the kid behind the counter and shove a handful of popcorn in my mouth as I turn away, anxious to get into the darkened theater before anyone can see the tears forming in my eyes.

And I nearly run into Dave, who is staring at me like I just shot his puppy.

I swallow my mouthful of popcorn. "Sorry, I didn't see you."

Dave grabs a jumbo tub of popcorn and a large drink from the counter and shakes his head, his lips pressed together into a tight smile. "Enjoy your movie," he says. "I hope it's everything you expected it to be."

Then, he and his cousin disappear through the same doors that swallowed up Jarod and Laina.

Living in the shadow of perfection really sucks.

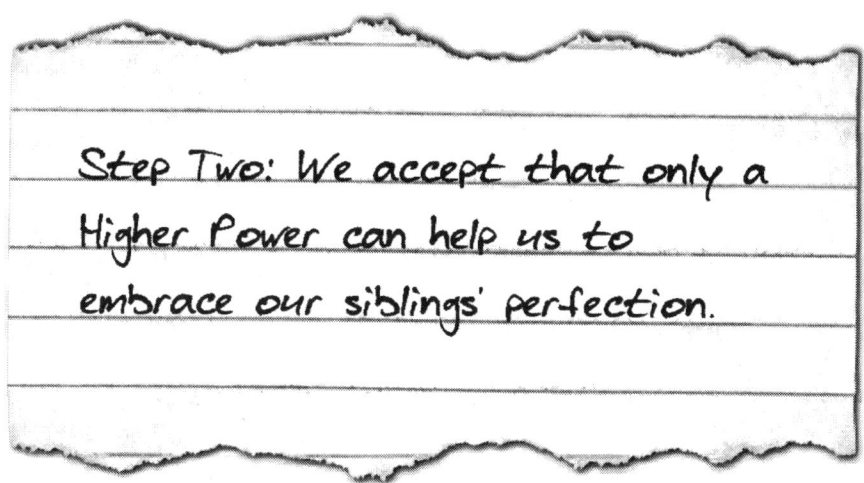

Chapter Four

Laina surveys the piles of clothing stacked haphazardly on a collection of folding tables in our basement, and then she turns her attention to the five of us who have volunteered to help. She turns on her dazzling smile, and I can practically hear Jarod panting beside me.

"Okay, this is a big job," Laina says, "but if we divide and conquer, we can get it done quickly." She glances at the clipboard in her hand. "Andi was kind enough to put together a checklist for us, and she divided the work up to make it a little bit more manageable. So this should all run much more smoothly than last year. Even though there are fewer of us this time around, if we stick to the schedule, we should be able to finish it all in one day."

Everyone cheers and I force myself not to roll my eyes. Helping her coordinate the clothing drive isn't exactly my favorite way to spend the Saturday before Valentine's Day, but I'm still walking on eggshells with my parents over my biology grade, and I can use all the look-at-how-responsible-I-am brownie points I can get. And I'm hoping to earn some points with Jarod, too.

Besides, Laina is an organizational nightmare. She may be practically perfect in every way, but she's more of a big-idea dreamer than a put-the-plan-into-action leader. When Laina started the annual drive as her freshman service project three years ago, I didn't think she'd be able to keep it all organized, but her compulsive perfectionism kicked in and kept the whole thing running fairly smoothly. And when Ms. Detweiler urged her to do it all again her sophomore year, she pulled it off with no problem.

But the clothing drive has gotten bigger every year, and Laina's natural disorganization has gotten worse lately. Last year, she didn't even get all of the clothes sorted and distributed for weeks after the collection day. She totally needs my help, so she doesn't end up doing everything by herself while her "volunteers" stand around eating donuts and ogling her, like they do every year.

"Okay, Andi has broken the job into three easy tasks," Laina says. "As coordinator, and point of contact for the drive, naturally I'll be the one to call the shelter and the domestic abuse safe house to collect their final wish lists, so that we can prioritize the division of donations between them." She glances at her clipboard again. "While I'm doing that, I need two of you to start sorting the clothes we've already collected, and the other three can pick up the clothes from the remaining donation drop-off points." She holds up the map I drew and points to the sixteen little stars. "When you get back with the last of the donations, we can all work together to finish the final sorting, and then we can divide the clothes between the sites, according to their needs."

Laina looks up, expectantly, but the guys just stare at her blankly, waiting for her to tell them what to do.

I move to a table behind Laina. "I'll start sorting." I've

already mapped out a plan for going through the piles, and I figure I can get this batch sorted long before the others return with the rest of the donations.

Jarod strolls over and grabs a pair of ratty boxer shorts from the top of the pile. "Please tell me we're not sending things like this to the shelter," he says, crinkling his nose.

Laina laughs. "Of course not. All used underwear and ripped or stained clothes can go into that trash can for recycling." She looks at the three remaining volunteers. "Are you boys okay with going to pick up the rest of the donations?"

Rob nods. "We've got it."

"Actually," Dave says, "I was thinking I might be better at sorting. I'm pretty good at organizing things, and I think Andi and I would make a great team." He strolls over to the mountain of clothes on the table and starts pawing through the pile.

Laina frowns and consults the plan I outlined for her. "No, we already have two people sorting, and we really need three of you to go pick up those other donations." She holds out two sheets of paper. "Here is the map, and here is a list of contacts for each location. Let them know you're with me, and that you're picking up the final donations."

Dave frowns. "Jarod can go with these guys."

I shake my head. "If you're not willing to help, why are you even here? Don't you have your little cousin to take care of or something?"

"Nope. They left this morning. And I will help. We can do the sorting." He grabs a handful of t-shirts from the table and glances at each one before tossing it back into the pile.

"Sorry, this job's already taken." Jarod winks at me and bumps my shoulder playfully. "We've got this, right?"

"As long as you follow my plan, it'll be a piece of cake." I duck my head to conceal the blush creeping up on my cheeks.

Dave takes the pages from Laina, glaring at Jarod as he backs away from the table. "Do we really need three people to pick up donations? It looks like there's a lot of stuff to sort here. Maybe I should stay." He hands the pages to Rob and looks at Laina with sad, puppy dog eyes.

"We have sixteen donation sites to cover," she says. "And we have to get them all today. I think Andi and Jarod will be fine."

Rob grabs his keys and consults the map, and Dave yanks his coat off the back of his chair, shoving his arms into the sleeves before stomping up the stairs.

"We'll be back before you know it," Josh says. He and Rob follow Dave, and a moment later, I hear Rob's truck pulling out of the driveway.

"You got this?" Laina asks me.

"Yeah, we're good," Jarod says. "Andi's already got a system all worked out." I blush and he laughs. "See? No problem."

Laina hugs us both. "I'll be upstairs if you need me," she says. Then, she races upstairs to start making phone calls.

"Tell me your master plan, oh wise one." Jarod bows in mock reverence. "What do we do first?"

I pull a second folding table over and arrange the tables to form a U-shape with the couch, placing the trash can between the tables at the top of the U. Then, I grab an armful of clothes and dump them onto the couch.

"First, we consolidate all of these little piles into one central location. We can do a quick, rough sort, putting the boys' clothes here and the girls' clothes over there, and tossing out anything that isn't in good shape or is just plain gross." I grab the ratty boxers Jarod is still holding and toss them into the trash can. "We can do a detailed sort after that."

"What if we find something really snazzy and we want to keep it for ourselves?" Jarod pulls the ugliest lime green and hot pink Hawaiian-style shirt I've ever seen out of the pile. The shirt is ginormous and gaudy, but otherwise in good shape. We'll keep it in the donation pile, because there's nothing technically wrong with it, but I wouldn't wish a shirt like that on my worst enemy. He slips it on and flexes his muscles, but the shirt is so huge that it still looks like he's swimming in a sea of hideous fashion sense.

I laugh and fish a thick, orange and avocado green, scratchy woolen scarf and a rainbow striped belt out of the pile. "Your ensemble is missing something, dahling," I say in my best snobby fashionista voice. I buckle the belt around his waist and reach up to wind the scarf around his neck.

My fingers brush against the stubble on his cheek, and I shiver as a jolt of electricity shoots up my arm, but Jarod is too busy rummaging through the pile to notice. He pulls out a pair of purple plaid shorts and pulls them on over his jeans, and then he struts across the room like a runway model.

I laugh and clap. "Brilliant! That outfit is so you!"

Jarod bows and then he saunters back to the pile of clothing still to be sorted. He holds up a long, velvet dress. "Hey, do you know what this reminds me of?" he asks.

I nod. "*Much Ado About Nothing*, right? That looks almost like the dress I had to wear." I pull it out of his hands and inspect it briefly before tossing it onto the "girls" pile. "Except mine had a broken zipper." I laugh, remembering the awkward way I had to slide across the stage, careful never to turn my back to the audience, so they wouldn't know about my wardrobe malfunction.

"But you pulled it off," Jarod says. "No one even knew you weren't fully-clothed. Except for those of us who had to stare at your bare back onstage every night." He grins and digs back into the pile of clothes. "Do you still wear a Hello Kitty bra? Or have you graduated to Dora the Explorer?"

I roll my eyes and busy myself with the clothes to hide the blush creeping up on my cheeks. "So you've spent the last six years daydreaming about me in my underwear? That's a little bit creepy, don't you think?"

Jarod turns a brilliant shade of red. "That's not what I meant."

I laugh. "Relax. I know I flashed the whole cast on a nightly basis. Probably pretty hard to forget. But I think it's pretty obvious that you weren't paying attention. I never wore Hello Kitty. Strictly Wonder Woman."

We quickly paw through the rest of the clothes, tossing them into "his," "hers," and "trash" piles, finishing the preliminary sort in almost no time. Even though we keep everything that isn't ripped, stained or disgusting, I'm amazed at how much we have to throw away. The trash bin is already more than half full, and this is only from the clothing collected at school.

"Don't people realize this is supposed to be stuff for actual people to wear?" I ask. "If we wanted to collect trash, we would have applied to be sanitation workers instead."

"What? You're kidding me." Jarod shakes his head, his eyes sparkling with amusement. "Your problem is that you're too picky. If you weren't throwing away so many treasures, we wouldn't have such a big trash pile." He grins and pulls a shredded pair of jeans from the garbage can. "You don't think someone will want these? You're into fashion. Didn't you know that the ripped denim look is really hot right now?"

I laugh. "Um, I'm not exactly into fashion, Jar. I'm more interested in looking good. Can I help it if I have a talent for that?" I push my fist through the massive hole right next to the zipper. "Showing a little skin on the knee, or even the back, is one thing, but no one really wants to see this much!"

"Oh, come on. Now you're being judgmental. How do you know what other people want to see and what they don't?" He digs through to the bottom of the trash bin until he finds that old, ratty pair of boxer shorts. "Well, look at that. It's a perfectly matched set," he says. "I could wear this ensemble to my next college admissions interview and make a really good first impression."

Jarod could totally pull off the ripped denim look. With his super-confident swagger, I bet he could even get away with wearing something like that for an actual interview and not blow it. I glance at the torn jeans in his hands and imagine them wrapped around his muscular legs, the tight denim hugging the perfect shape of his butt, the tears and slashes revealing his perfectly-toned thighs …

I blush and grab the jeans out of his hands, quickly burying them under several layers of trashed clothes and breathing deeply to bring my pulse back to normal. I'm cool and unruffled and in control. "Yeah, I'd love to see that," I say.

Jarod reaches into the bin and grabs a handful of black fabric from the top of the pile. "And I would love to see you in this." He holds the item up and gives it a little shake to unfold it. My eyes about pop out of my head when I see that he's displaying a tiny, black nightgown that wouldn't have covered much skin, even before someone ripped the entire lace front to shreds.

My stomach flips as I imagine modeling that nightgown for him, but I raise one eyebrow and lean against the table. "Still fantasizing about me in my underwear, huh?" I ask.

Jarod glances at his hand and the color drains from his face.

"Not that I blame you, or anything. I am pretty hot." I flip my hair over my shoulder and strike a pose.

Jarod drops the lingerie back into the bin. "I meant this," he mumbles, pulling out a torn Guns N' Roses t-shirt that's missing one sleeve. His face burns a brilliant shade of crimson. "They're both black. Easy mistake."

I grab the nightgown and hold it up in front of me. "Are you sure?" I ask. "I bet I'd look amazing in something like this."

He gulps and looks away, sweat beading on his forehead. "You're too young for that," he says, yanking the nightgown out of my hands and tossing it into the trash bin. "Stick with Guns N' Roses."

I take the vintage t-shirt from him and set it aside. With the missing sleeve and torn hem, it's not exactly something I'd pass on to the shelter for the clothing drive, but I might actually be able to make it work. I'm keeping it.

I turn to the piles of pre-sorted clothing, determined to keep myself busy, so I won't slip up and say something I'll regret. "We still have to sort these by size and style."

"Right." He joins me at the table. "Stop playing around and get to work."

I grin and bump against him with my shoulder, taking a deep breath to still the butterflies that kick up in my stomach when we touch. "I'm sorry if you can't concentrate, but you can't just turn off beauty and charm like mine. I don't blame you for fantasizing about me." I glance pointedly at the trash bin.

He blushes. "What? No, that could've happened to anyone."

I nod thoughtfully. "You're right. Guys fantasize about me all the time." I wave my hand in front of myself. "Ahem. Smokin' hot, remember?"

Jarod laughs and smacks himself in the forehead. "Oh yeah. How could I forget?"

"I'll forgive you this one time," I say, "as long as you don't ever forget such an important fact again." I sigh dramatically in a way that hopefully says "I'm totally playing right now" and not "why won't you love me?"

"Okay, it's a deal." He shakes my hand, holding it just a bit longer than necessary, and for the tiniest flicker of an instant, I think I see a glimmer of interest in Jarod's eyes. But before the tension between us can develop into anything more than the barest hint of a spark, the door opens and Laina skips down the stairs.

"Hey guys, how's it coming down here?" She glances at the piles of clothes and shakes her head slowly. "I kind of expected you to be nearly finished by now, but it doesn't look like you've done much of anything. Andi, you said you were going to help. I can't have you distracting my volunteers."

Jarod blushes and moves away, as if the air around me is suddenly toxic.

Like everything else about Laina, her timing is absolutely perfect.

Chapter Five

A sharp knock at the front door makes me jump, and I spill milk all over the homework I'm trying to convince myself to complete. I toss a towel over the soggy mess and glance through the window next to the door.

Jarod.

I run my fingers through my hair and straighten my sweater. And I tell my heart to stop fluttering. He's not here for me. He's been avoiding me since the clothing drive. He barely looked at me when our family sat next to his at church on Sunday, and he didn't even say hello when he came to pick Laina up for their annual I-hate-Valentine's-day dinner last night.

I take a deep breath and open the door. If he's still embarrassed, the best thing is to act like Saturday never even happened.

I'm good at pretending.

"Um, Laina's not home from school yet," I say. "I thought she stayed after to hang out with you at play practice."

Jarod grimaces. "She did."

"Well, you beat her home. Do you want to come in? She should be here any minute."

"She left over an hour ago," he says. "I had to go over some issues with the stage manager, and then Mr. Finn wanted to talk to me about the lighting for the big musical number."

I frown and glance over his shoulder at the street. "Maybe she stopped at the library or she had to get gas or something? Or maybe that old clunker of hers broke down on the side of the road?"

"No. I would have seen her." Jarod glares at Laina's empty parking space. "We were supposed to study tonight, but then that creep, Crawford, asked her to drive him home. An hour ago."

"I don't think I know anyone named Crawford. Is he new?"

Jarod growls. "You know, Crawford. Arrogant. Egomaniac. Star of every school play since kindergarten. Thinks he's God's gift to the world. Pain in my a— in my butt."

I smile. Laina has this strict no-swearing rule that she expects everyone to follow, and Jarod is usually pretty good about it, except when he's all worked up. It's kind of cute to watch him stumbling all over himself to follow her rules, even when she's not around to notice.

But I still don't know anyone named Crawford. "Are you sure I've met him?"

"You know, Shane Crawford. Used to be my best friend, until I realized that he didn't care about anyone besides himself?"

Oh. Shane. The guy Laina's been lusting after for the last three years, ever since Jarod introduced them to each other.

"You mean Rachel's boyfriend? If he's so horrible, why did you give him the lead in your play?"

Jarod frowns. "I didn't. Mr. Finn wanted him, and faculty advisor trumps student director." He glances back at the empty street, as if he expects Laina to magically appear. "And it's not that I hate Crawford. He's not even worth the effort. I just don't trust him."

I bite my lip and step back, pulling Jarod into the house. "Don't worry. I'm sure Laina's totally safe." I take Jarod's hand and lead him into the living room, and I say a little prayer. But I'm not sure if I should ask God to make Laina hurry home, or if I should ask Him to keep her out for a while longer.

It's not like anything is going to actually happen between Shane and Laina. She's too clueless to realize that he has a crush on her too, and he's too stupid to make his move. They've been stuck in this endless loop of almost-flirting for years, and instead of asking her out, Shane started dating Rachel Nichols, Emily's sister and Laina's ex-best friend, a few months ago. I'm pretty sure he was trying to make Laina jealous, but instead it totally killed any chance he might have had with my sister. Miss Perfect would never do anything with her friend's boyfriend, even if they haven't actually been friends since Kendra wormed her way in between them back in seventh grade.

"You know how scatterbrained Laina is," I say. "She probably started talking and lost track of time. I'm pretty sure Shane has a cell phone, so if they had some kind of car trouble, you know she'd call. And I haven't heard anything from her."

Jarod scowls. "That's what I'm afraid of."

"What?"

He looks at me and raises one eyebrow.

I shake my head. "No way."

"Crawford is really good at getting what he wants. And he wants Laina."

"He has a girlfriend, remember? Rachel? Head

cheerleader and second most popular girl in the senior class?"

"Yeah, like that's going to stop him."

"It would stop Laina."

"Yeah, but Crawford's devious. He'll try something, and she won't even know it's coming. I should never have let her go. I can't protect her if I'm not there."

"Okay, that's it." I jump up and grab my coat from the front hall closet, and then I grab Jarod's hand to pull him outside. "Let's go."

He hesitates. "Do you really think we should? I don't want her to think I don't trust her."

"No, you moron." I shiver and wrap my fuzzy pink scarf around my neck. "We're not looking for Laina. She's a big girl, and she can take care of herself."

"But what if ..."

"No." I walk to Jarod's car and wait for him to unlock the door. Laina may be semi-clueless when it comes to real life, but she's not stupid. "We're not sitting around here while you imagine all kinds of worst-case scenarios. Before you do something dumb and totally ruin your friendship, we're going to a movie. Something with plenty of action and shooting and not a hint of romance."

Jarod opens the door for me. "Yeah. She'll call when she gets home, right?"

I shake my head and hold out my hand. "Give me your phone. You can't come running the second she calls. You have to give her a chance to miss you."

He reluctantly hands over his phone, and I silence it before slipping it into my purse. "Trust me, we'll have fun."

"I guess so." Jarod shrugs and turns on the car. "Maybe we can see *Superheroes in Space*?"

"Perfect."

I insist that we go to the Cinema Twelve Theater on the other side of town, because everyone always goes to the Super Seven at the mall. There won't be any Laina-related memories associated with The Twelve. Besides, it's far enough from our house that I should have plenty of time to work my magic.

After a twenty-minute drive and my very best attempts to distract him, Jarod is actually smiling by the time he buys our tickets.

I claim the perfect seats, right in the center of the fourteenth row, while Jarod waits in the concessions line to buy popcorn and Junior Mints. As soon as I sit down, I slip his phone out of my purse and check for missed calls. Sure enough, there's a call from our home phone number that came in less than five minutes ago.

Jarod's password isn't hard to guess. Of course he would choose Laina's birthdate. I glance over my shoulder to make sure Jarod isn't sneaking up behind me as I listen to the voicemail.

"Jarod, I'm not feeling well. Can we study tomorrow night instead?" Laina sniffles in her my-life-is-falling-apart-and-I-need-you-to-rescue-me voice. Which probably means that she's realized once again how stupid it is to harbor a smoldering crush on someone else's boyfriend. She obviously wants her best friend to remind her that she's beautiful and perfect and to tell her she deserves better than a guy like Shane Crawford. And the second Jarod hears this message, he'll go running straight to her rescue.

But I worked too hard to put a smile back on his face.

I delete the voicemail and erase our phone number from the missed calls list, and then slip the phone back into my purse seconds before Jarod finds me in the semi-darkened theater.

Jarod hands me a soda and a giant bucket of popcorn as he slides into the seat beside me. "Did I miss any good previews?" He tears open a box of Junior Mints and dumps them on top of the popcorn, giving the tub a little shake to mix it together.

I nod and grab a handful of the salty-and-sweet popcorn mix. "Oh yeah. There was this one about a dancing candy box and his love affair with a giant cup of soda. Totally a Romeo and Juliet kind of thing. I didn't catch the name of the movie, but we should definitely plan to see that one next time. I think it was called 'Visit our Concession Stand' or something."

Jarod laughs. "Only if they play it in 3-D with smell-o-vision technology."

"Oh, look. It's playing now." I toss a handful of popcorn at him, and instead of ducking, he opens his mouth.

"Yum! Best movie of the season. Two thumbs up."

The lady behind us kicks my seat and clears her throat loudly as the opening credits play. I lean over to whisper in Jarod's ear. "I guess she doesn't agree with your review of the feature. She must not be a big fan of foodie films."

Jarod laughs and angry lady shushes us again. I bury my face in Jarod's shoulder to stifle a giggle. He squeezes my hand and grins at me.

When he releases my hand, he doesn't pull away completely, and for the rest of the movie, whenever I shift in my seat, our fingers brush against each other. I'm afraid he'll hear my heart pounding, even over the sound of the exploding planets and laser blasts as the Superheroes in Space battle the evil forces of C.O.D.E. (the Confederation of Dastardly Evil).

When the movie is over, I excuse myself while the closing credits roll and race to the bathroom to check Jarod's phone again. There's only one missed call.

From Shane Crawford.

I check the messages, but there are none. Shane had to know that Jarod won't call him back without a really good reason. I hesitate briefly, wondering why Shane would call Jarod at all. It might be an innocent question about the school play that only Jarod could answer, but Jarod might think that the call was from Laina, and I'm not about to let one phone call ruin all my hard work.

Delete.

Jarod is waiting for me when I emerge from the bathroom, so I smile and reapply my carefully constructed carefree attitude. "Did I miss anything funny at the end of the closing credits?"

"Just cranky lady storming out of the theater in a huff when I asked her if her movie-going experience was a pleasant one."

I laugh. "I wish I'd been there to see the look on her face!" I loop my arm through his and pull him out of the theater. "See? I told you this was a good idea." Jarod doesn't ask for his phone, and I'm careful not to mention my sister's name. He doesn't need any reminders.

Chapter Six

Jarod unlocks and opens the door for me. When he smiles, I have to remind myself that this is not a date, only two friends hanging out on a random afternoon.

But that's a start.

"I'm not really ready to go home yet," Jarod says as he slips behind the wheel. "Want to go out for ice cream or something?"

I watch the snow swirling around the parking lot and shiver. This is totally not ice cream weather, and I know he's only suggesting it because he and Laina have this crazy tradition about eating ice cream when it's really cold outside. Laina says ice cream in warm weather is too cliché.

"I could go for something sweet," I say, "but how about a piece of warm apple pie at Mona's instead? Or we could go to Eileen's Cookies and see if they have any that are fresh out of the oven."

Jarod starts the car and pulls out of the parking lot. "I

know the perfect place. You don't mind taking a little drive with me, do you?"

I shake my head. He grins and my stomach flips. I don't know how Laina can possibly stand to spend so much time in close proximity to that smile and not fall completely head-over-heels in love with him. Sure, Shane is totally charming, and he has that sexy, gravelly voice that makes everyone swoon, but he's nothing compared to Jarod.

We pull onto the highway and head south, away from town. Jarod cranks up the heater and the radio, and I lean back in my seat to watch the snow silently rushing by outside.

"Where are we going?" I ask half an hour later, as we drive past the last sign of civilization and into the nothingness of a Wyoming interstate highway. The sun sets behind the mountains, and the only light for miles is the light coming from our headlights. There aren't even any other cars on the road. "Is this some elaborate scheme to get me alone so you can take advantage of my innocence?"

"Of course it is," Jarod says with a smirk. "That's the kind of guy I am."

"And what kind of a girl do you think I am?" I can't suppress a grin, so my attempt at a serious, scolding voice is totally lost.

"Well, you know, I was hoping ..." By the dim light of the instrument panel, I see Jarod wiggling his eyebrows, and he gives me a look that might be a feeble attempt at "seductive," but he can't keep a straight face either, and he ends up laughing instead.

My heart thumps, and I clasp my hands in my lap so I won't reach for him. We're only joking, but he's never looked at me this way before. Suddenly, I don't feel like Laina's awkward little sister anymore.

"Is this because I didn't model that black, lace thingamawhatsit for you last weekend?" I tilt my head slightly and look at him thoughtfully. "You've been fantasizing about it ever since, haven't you? And now you think you can lure me out here to the middle of nowhere under false pretenses and the promise of a sumptuous dessert, so you can have your way with me."

Jarod inhales sharply and gives me a look I can't quite interpret before he chuckles. "You figured it out. I guess you're too smart for me. I've been fantasizing about ravaging you ever since we got interrupted last Saturday. You're all I can think about. You fill my every thought. You are my one and only desire."

For a moment, I forget that he's kidding around. I hold my breath, waiting for him to reach for me, wondering if I should make the first move.

"Well, you and these incredible hot fudge brownie sundaes, of course." Jarod pulls off the interstate and into the completely empty parking lot of a run-down hole-in-the-wall truck stop with a broken neon sign flashing "Yes, we're open" in the window. Except, every other letter is burned out, so it really says "Ys er pe."

It's not exactly a romantic destination. More like a hangout for serial killers. But I can't imagine Laina ever willingly eating here, which means I'm not sharing the experience with her memory.

"Are you sure?" I clutch my seatbelt and sink into my seat. "It's a little ... scary, isn't it?"

Jarod squeezes my hand. "Don't worry. I'll protect you." He jumps out and rushes around to my side of the car to open the door for me. "Trust me. You'll love it." He pulls me from the car, and I hold his hand tightly as we walk through the snow to the run-down diner.

A rusty cowbell on a string clangs to announce our arrival as we walk in, and I blink in the slightly-too-bright florescent light. I take a deep breath, savoring the aroma of greasy fries and chili, mixed with warm apple pie. With the cracked red vinyl booths and chipped Formica tabletops, combined with the soft strains of "Help me, Rhonda" playing in the background, I feel like I've stepped through a time warp to the fifties. I feel like I should be wearing a poodle skirt and a ponytail.

Jarod smiles and waves at the waitress. "Hey, Amy! Can I get the usual? And one for my girl here, too." He winks at me. "She's a first-timer, so let's make it extra special, okay?"

Amy, a slender brunette with a mischievous twinkle in her brown eyes that matches the glint in Jarod's, laughs and ducks behind the counter. "Anything for my favorite guy," she says. "Sit anywhere you want, and I'll have that right out for you."

Jarod doesn't let go of my hand until we're sitting on the cushioned seat of a corner booth. "See? Nothing to be afraid of."

I slide closer to Jarod and shiver slightly. "Well, not yet, but I reserve the right to jump into your lap and cower in terror if Amy suddenly morphs into a flesh-eating creature from another planet."

"My lap is ready and waiting for you whenever you need it," Jarod says. "As long as you don't try to take my ice cream, we'll be fine."

Amy appears and sets two gigantic dessert dishes on the table. A brownie nearly as big as a dinner plate is piled with a mountain of cookies 'n cream ice cream and drenched with hot fudge, then topped with whipped cream, nuts, and a maraschino cherry. It's the kind of dessert usually advertised as a "sundae for two." Laina would have a heart attack at the thought of eating even a quarter of this monster sundae. I love that Jarod doesn't even bat an eyelash when I polish off the whole thing before stealing a few bites from his dish.

"Here, I saved this part for you," he says, scooping up a small pile of candied pecans and whipped cream. I open my mouth and he feeds them to me, and then he traces my lower lip with his thumb. "You had a little bit of whipped cream right there."

If it was anyone else, I'd definitely say he was flirting with me, but my guy-reading abilities get totally scrambled when Jarod is involved. I pull away and scoop up the last bite of his brownie to give my mouth something to do.

Jarod doesn't like nuts, so of course he would let me eat them. And he wouldn't want me to walk around all night with a glob of whipped cream stuck to my lip. He's not flirting. The last time I thought Jarod was hitting on me, he was only working up the nerve to ask for my help with Laina.

I refuse to get my hopes up again.

We chat casually on our way home, discussing favorite ice cream flavors and science according to *Superheroes in Space*. (Who knew regular humans could breathe normally in the vacuum of space, as long as they were holding hands with a superhero while flying between planets?)

Laina's name doesn't pop up even once.

When we pull up in front of my house, I can see that her car is in its usual space, but the house is dark, so I'm guessing she went to bed early. She won't be sitting around, ready to ask Jarod why he didn't call her back. And by tomorrow, she'll be too embarrassed about the call to bring it up, so he'll never know I messed with his phone.

Jarod walks me to the front door, steadying me when I slip on a patch of black ice. He doesn't pull away when I've regained my balance, and I can feel his heart thumping in rhythm with my own through our heavy coats. I stare up into his soft, green eyes and when he smiles, I can't help imagining the way his lips would feel against mine.

"Do you want to come inside for a little bit?" I ask, hoping both that he'll say yes and that he won't. I want him to want to spend more time with me, but everything I've worked for tonight will be ruined if Laina isn't asleep yet.

Jarod shakes his head. "I'd better get home. I already kept you out past your curfew."

I glance at my watch. It's only ten, which would be fine on a weekend, but it's Tuesday, and my dad has this crazy idea that Laina and I should be ready for bed by eight-thirty on school nights. But Dad's car isn't in the driveway, and I don't see a light in their bedroom window, so Mom and Dad must have gone out.

"I think we're okay," I say.

Jarod glances from the door to the driveway and back at me. He's thinking about it. But then he shakes his head. "I'd better go." He bites his lower lip. "But I'll see you tomorrow."

I slip my hands around his neck, burying my fingers in his hair. Before I can stop to think about what I'm doing, I lean in for a kiss.

Jarod turns away a fraction of a second before our lips meet. "We can't."

He glances toward the house, and I close my eyes, cursing my impulsiveness. I've totally ruined everything I worked so hard for tonight. But then he touches my cheek and I open my eyes again. He smiles. "We shouldn't," he says, and brushes his lips against mine, so quickly I almost don't feel it.

He traces the contours of my lips and my cheek with his thumb. "You're so beautiful." He catches my lower lip between his teeth, and his tongue traces my upper lip.

I let out an involuntary moan, and he pulls me close, the kiss deepening. His lips move across my cheek to my neck, and he nibbles playfully as he pushes me up against the front door, his body tight against mine. I run my fingers through his hair and take a gasping breath as I recapture his lips.

After an eternity, we break apart and Jarod takes a staggering step back. "Wow," he says. "That was ... wow."

"Yeah." I press my hand to my chest to still my racing heart, waiting for him to kiss me again. When I can't stand it anymore, I take a step closer and he reaches out to caress my cheek, but then headlights wash over us as Dad's car pulls into the driveway.

Jarod stumbles down the porch steps and races across the street to his car. He unlocks the door, then stops and turns back toward me. I raise my hand to my lips to blow him a kiss, and I freeze that way when he calls, "Good night, Laina! I'll see you tomorrow!"

I stagger into the house and down the hall to my bedroom, where I lock the door and crawl into bed without even undressing. I ignore the knock when Mom and Dad come to say goodnight, and I bury my face in my pillow so that no one can hear my sobs.

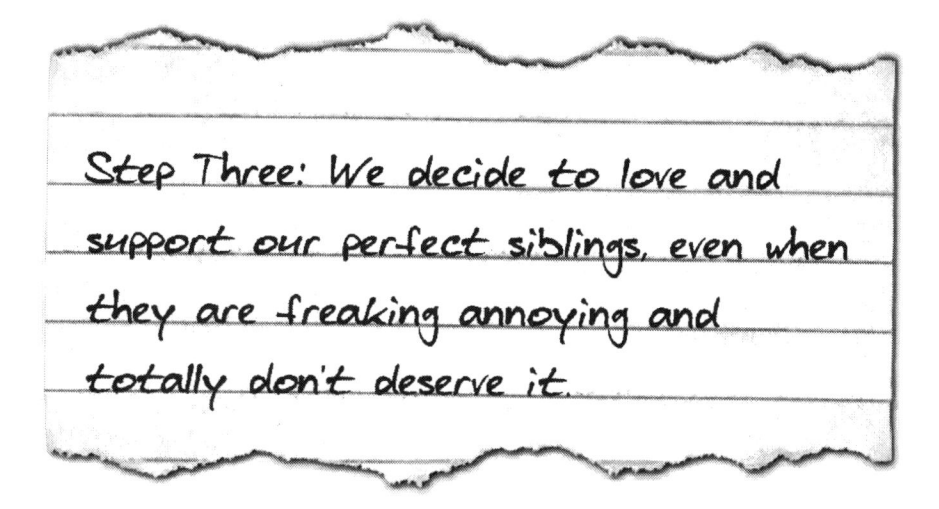

Step Three: We decide to love and support our perfect siblings, even when they are freaking annoying and totally don't deserve it.

Chapter Seven

Laina mopes around the house for the next week. Other than school, which she wouldn't miss even if she was legitimately dying, because it might damage her perfect GPA, Laina refuses to go anywhere or talk to anyone. She spends most of her time curled up in bed, scribbling furiously in her diary. She won't talk to Kendra. She even stops trying to micromanage my life.

I haven't seen Laina this depressed since the state marching band tournament last year, when she tripped on the stairs and tore her uniform right before we had to perform. She blamed herself for ruining the formation and killing our chance to win the trophy, even though everyone knew we only lost because that jerk, Anthony, totally bailed and left a gaping hole in the line.

For months afterward, Laina wouldn't talk to anyone except Jarod. She slept all the time, and her grades slipped from A-plusses to A-minuses. But when she finally snapped out of it, her perfectionism kicked into high gear.

Two years ago, she never would have told mom about my occasional vacations from biology, but now she's constantly looking over my shoulder, trying to turn me into a clone of herself. Ironically, the more Laina tries to make everything fit into her idea of perfection, the sloppier she gets in private. You can barely see her bedroom floor anymore, through all the piles of clothes and stacks of books.

She's acting like the sky is falling all over again, but this time she's even avoiding Jarod. And I don't even want to think about the militant perfectionist she'll become when she gets over it this time.

Jarod calls almost every day, and Laina refuses to talk to him, which means I have to. I keep waiting for him to mention the kiss, but he doesn't. And I'm not about to bring it up.

Laina used to tell me everything, before she got all weird last year, and I keep hoping she'll snap out of this and talk to me like she used to, but by Saturday night, I'm tired of waiting.

I barge into Laina's room while she's getting dressed for the winter band concert. "I can't find my white shirt," I say. "Did you borrow it?"

Laina would never borrow my shirt. There's no way she could squeeze her DD-cups into a shirt that hugs my barely-there curves. But she isn't really listening to me anyway, so it doesn't matter what I say.

"No, I haven't seen your shoes. Do you want to borrow mine?"

"Not my shoes. I'm *wearing* my shoes, see?"

"Oh, good, you found them." She pulls her hair up into the tight bun we're required to wear for concerts.

I step fully into her room and close the door behind me. "I said I can't find my shirt. Can I look for it in your closet?" I reach into her closet and grab the shirt I'd planted there before dinner. "Oh, here it is." I pull off my t-shirt and slip on the frilly, white, tuxedo-style shirt. "As long as I'm in here, we should just get ready together."

Laina dumps her purse out on her bed and paws through the contents. "Have you seen my purple sparkly pen? The one I use when I write in my diary? I could have sworn I put it in my purse, but it's missing." She eyes me suspiciously. "You didn't take it, did you?"

"No, I don't have your pen." I glance around her messy room. "It's probably buried in one of these piles of clothes or books. Do you want me to help you organize things so you can find it? It'll take us twenty minutes. Thirty tops. And it will give us time to talk."

Maybe she can explain to me why the chronic neat freak has turned into a total slob.

Laina freezes, all the color draining from her face and her eyes widening in a classic deer-in-the-headlights look. She takes a deep breath, gives me a totally fake, forced smile, and shakes her head. "No, it's not really important anyway." She scoops the mess of pencils and crumpled papers, empty gum wrappers and breath mints back into her purse. Then she stares at it as if waiting for her favorite pen to speak to her.

"So anything new and exciting in your world lately?" I ask again.

Laina picks up her flute. "I'm sorry," she says, refusing to meet my eyes. "I want to get to school a little bit early so I can warm up and go over my solo one last time with Ms. Harmony. Can you get a ride with Mom and Dad?" She nods as if she's given me time to actually respond. "Good. Thanks! I'll see you in a bit, then."

She rushes through the door and out to her car before I even have time to remind her that Dad has his monthly schmooze-with-the-boss dinner tonight, and Mom and Dad aren't even coming to this concert. I pick up the phone and take a deep breath as I start punching in numbers. I hope

Summer doesn't mind giving me a ride.

I watch Laina throughout the concert, as she nervously stares at a particular spot in the third row of seats. Shane Crawford is watching her with the same intensity that I usually watch Jarod. And every time she glances at Shane, Laina misses notes and flubs her rhythms. She's wearing an I-totally-screwed-up look, but I'm positive it has nothing to do with the notes she's missing onstage, and everything to do with the way Shane's staring at her.

When my first long rest comes up, I lay my clarinet across my lap and casually brush the hair away from my eyes, surreptitiously stealing a glance at Jarod in the percussion section. I don't think he can see Shane from his position behind the drums at the back of the stage. Good. The last thing I need is to send Jarod into over-protective, jealous quasi-boyfriend mode again.

As soon as the concert is over, I race to the band room and throw my clarinet into its case. I'm already back to the auditorium and elbowing my way through the crowd to the third row before Laina leaves the stage.

Shane is so absorbed in watching my sister carefully stack her music together that he doesn't see me approaching. I drag him by the elbow through the side door to the empty back parking lot, where we can talk undisturbed, carefully propping the door open a crack so that we won't be locked outside.

"What's up with you and Laina?"

"Why? What did she say?"

I roll my eyes. "She hasn't *said* anything. But Laina has never missed a note outside of private practice in her life. Not until tonight. What did you do to my sister?"

Shane shuffles his feet and shoves his hands into his pockets, refusing to meet my eyes. "I only want to talk. To set things right." He pulls a purple, sparkly pen out of his pocket and studies it. "I thought if I could just ..."

"Hey!" I snatch the pen out of his hands. "Laina was totally searching for this."

He blushes. "She dropped it after chemistry."

"Okay, first of all, you're an idiot," I say. "If you want to apologize for whatever creeptastic thing you did, stealing Laina's pen and then giving it back to her isn't going to cut it." I shove the pen into my coat pocket.

Shane frowns. "But I need to explain."

"Well, whatever it is, I think you need to find a better way. Stalking her at a band concert and messing up her concentration isn't gonna work." I walk back to the auditorium door and yank it open. "Go home. And do yourself a favor. Wait until you have a better plan before you try again." I step into the crowded auditorium, pulling the door tightly closed behind me.

I manage to catch Laina before she can leave, so I don't have to find a ride home, but she's so quiet I might as well be in the car alone.

And when we get back to the house, Jarod is already waiting on our front porch for Laina and their annual post-winter-concert ice cream sundae tradition. She won't open up to me when Jarod's hanging around.

Especially not when Shane's the problem.

I smile and say hi, but Jarod's completely focused on Laina and doesn't even look at me. I storm into the house, to show that I don't care what, or even if, they think of me, but since neither of them appears to notice when I stalk off down the hall to my bedroom, the victory is kind of a hollow one.

I change out of my concert uniform, which looks good on absolutely no one, except maybe Jarod, and I slip into my favorite faded blue jeans that are torn in all of the right places and just happen to make my butt look amazing. I add a tight, turquoise tank top that totally brings out the color of my eyes and top it off with the old Guns N' Roses t-shirt.

Last Saturday, after the clothes were distributed to the various shelters, I spent the entire evening redesigning the shirt. I shortened the hem, slashed the remaining sleeve and widened the neckline. The result was a t-shirt that shows enough skin to make guys drool, without crossing the tramp line.

The outfit is sexy enough to get any red-blooded American boy's heart pumping, but it will mean a little bit more to Jarod. There's no way he'll be able to see me in this t-shirt without imagining that ripped nightgown.

I do a quick touch-up on my makeup and pull my hair out of its concert bun, carefully arranging my black curls to frame my face. Then, I take a deep breath and adopt my best "casually innocent" attitude before I saunter back to the kitchen.

"Great concert, guys! We rocked it!" I skip into the room and casually brush one finger along the back of Jarod's neck as I pass the table. He shivers at my touch and glances up at me. His jaw drops when he notices my outfit, but I pretend not to notice.

I fill the kettle with water, and then I set it on the stove to boil before I grab a package of Oreos from the cupboard and pull a chair up to the table between Jarod and Laina. "I don't see how you can eat ice cream when it's, like, fifteen degrees outside. What's wrong with you two?" I shiver and my knee "accidentally" brushes against Jarod's leg. I feel his body stiffen next to me, and I bite my lower lip to stifle a smile. "Don't you guys know ice cream makes you colder?"

Laina laughs and reaches across the table to squeeze Jarod's hand. "We always do this," she says. "It's tradition."

"Do you remember," Jarod asks, carefully avoiding my eyes, "when we were freshmen?" They launch into a story all about how they thought the juniors and seniors were going to the Dairy Shack for ice cream after their first concert, so they came back to our house to make ice cream sundaes. They thought they could tell everyone that they went out for ice cream and pretend they were a part of the cool kids, but then it turned out that everyone was really going out for brownies and hot cocoa instead.

The kettle whistles and I jump up to make my hot cocoa. I take a careful sip and return to my seat between them. "Really?" I ask. "You guys eat ice cream when it's freezing out because you were stupid when you were freshmen?" I lift my steaming mug and stare at Jarod over the cup as I take a sip. "I think I'd at least put a warm brownie with the ice cream."

"Oh, we have brownies and hot cocoa every year after the spring concert," Laina says. She's barely paying attention, and totally oblivious to the real conversation taking place right in front of her.

I pull my chair closer to Jarod, close enough that our legs are touching, and I eat the last bite of ice cream out of his dish. I lick my lips slowly, and then casually dunk an Oreo in my cocoa. "So the brownies and the ice cream are both because of Laina?"

Jarod squirms in his seat and glances at my sister, but she's a million miles away, absently rubbing at a sticky spot on the table with that vacant look on her face.

"It's just our thing," he says. "Because we're friends."

I give him a you-must-think-I'm-a-freaking-idiot smile and trace a figure eight with my index finger on his leg. He reaches under the table to grab my hand and looks at me with thinly veiled terror. I laugh and cock my head to one side, as if I'm only making casual conversation. "So, you would never, ever, for instance, eat brownies and ice cream *together* because Laina wouldn't approve?"

He blinks, and every trace of color drains from his face. His eyes plead with me to stop, and he squeezes my hand. But if he didn't want me to say anything in front of Laina, he shouldn't have avoided me all week.

"Or would the brownies and ice cream combination be a dangerous declaration that you wanted something way more than friendship?"

Jarod gulps and looks at Laina, who is still tracing hearts with her finger on the table. She nods absently.

"That's silly," he says. "It's a dessert. No symbols. No hidden meanings." He drops my hand and slides his chair away from me.

I take a deep breath and exhale slowly, folding my arms across my chest. "So when you eat them separately, the brownies and the ice cream are symbols of your enduring friendship. But when you eat them together, they mean nothing?"

"Sometimes a dessert is just a dessert," Jarod says.

I twist open an Oreo and slowly lick the cream filling. "What about kisses?" I ask. "Do those mean anything?"

Laina looks up with a start. "What?"

Jarod coughs and rakes his fingers through his hair. "Oh, we're talking about our favorite candies. I was thinking about the way something can be really good, but it's not always the best thing for you. Sometimes, you have to know when to walk away. And leave. It. Alone."

He reaches across the table and pats my arm, then turns his full attention to Laina, transitioning into a discussion of college plans and other unimportant nonsense.

I've been dismissed.

I fake a giggle. "You're totally right," I say.

"Sometimes, the bitter aftertaste is so repulsive that it's totally not worth it." I lock eyes with Jarod, determined not to let him see my pain. "Especially when the candy wasn't even any good in the first place."

Laina laughs. "Andi, you're such a junk food junkie. I can't imagine that you've ever tasted a candy you didn't like."

"She's got a point, you know." Jarod grins and traces the slashed sleeve of my t-shirt. He totally knows I picked this outfit for him. And he's laughing at me.

I suddenly want to hurt him, and I know exactly where to hit the hardest.

"Oh! I almost forgot!" I jump up and run to my bedroom. Laina's pen is still tucked safely away in my coat pocket. I wipe the tears from my eyes before they can escape and trail mascara down my cheeks, and then reapply my carefree attitude, before skipping back to the kitchen with a grin and a totally realistic giggle.

"Here, Laina," I say. "That Shane kid found me after the concert. He wanted you, but he had to go, so he asked me to give this to you, since you were taking forever to put away your flute." I roll my eyes and flip my hair. "He said you dropped it after class."

I giggle again and lock eyes with Jarod. Taking a deep breath, I remind myself to be cool and unruffled, not giggly and imbecilic. "How dumb does he think we are, right? Like anyone would ever sit through a boring high school band concert to return a pen." I widen my eyes innocently, and gasp as if I'm suddenly realizing the truth. "He took the pen when you weren't looking, so he'd have an excuse to come talk to you when he brought it back! Oh, my gondola, Laina! That's so sweet. He was *so* disappointed when he didn't see you after the concert." I sigh dramatically and clasp my hands over my heart. "How adorable is it that he would go through all that to spend a few minutes alone with you? He totally wants you."

Laina's knuckles go white as she clutches the pen. She bites her lip and tips her head forward so that her long, blonde hair falls in front of her eyes. Usually, she jumps at any hint that Shane might be interested in her, so I'm not expecting the panicked terror I catch in her expression. I immediately feel guilty for making her think about whatever Shane did to her, but there's no turning back now.

I lock eyes with Jarod. "I'd totally fall for a guy like that. One who isn't scared of his feelings."

Jarod frowns and looks out the window at the gently falling snow. "Wow, the storm is really getting bad out there. I guess I'd better go before the roads aren't safe."

"Are you kidding?" Laina asks. "It's barely even snowing. You drive in worse than this all the time."

"Yeah, but I promised my mom I'd stop and get some milk on the way home, and things might get really bad if I stay." He hugs Laina and glares at me. "I'll see you tomorrow."

He scurries outside, and I pop another Oreo into my mouth. It tastes like sawdust, but I force myself to swallow it with a smile. "What's his problem?" I think of the terrified look in Jarod's eyes when he realized that I could ruin his chances with Laina if I wanted to. The confidence and power I expected to feel sits mangled in my gut, buried under an avalanche of guilt. This wasn't the way I wanted to get his attention.

Laina frowns and waves her pen. "You couldn't wait to give this to me until after he left? You know how much he hates Shane."

"I thought you'd be happy. It seemed so important before the concert." I pop another Oreo into my mouth. Laina stares at the pen with a glassy, far-off expression, and I have to turn away. I intercepted Shane at the concert so he wouldn't hurt my sister again, but I hurt her worse than he could have. At least Laina knew she needed to be cautious with Shane. My attack came out of nowhere.

I shove the package of cookies behind a box of cereal in the pantry and take a deep breath. It's not my fault. If Jarod hadn't tried to ignore me all week, I never would have lashed out at him. And Laina doesn't need to be so sensitive.

"It's just a pen," I say, and saunter out of the room without waiting for her reply.

Chapter Eight

Laina's practicing her flute, playing the same passage of music over and over again until it's absolutely flawless. I shouldn't be surprised. Miss Perfect always stresses about the next performance, even when we have practically forever to get ready, and after messing up at the concert last weekend, she thinks the whole school is laughing at her. But this level of obsessive rehearsal is intense, even for her. I have to hum along a half-note off-key for a full minute before she finally gives up and puts her flute away.

"Okay," I say. "Time ran out on your pity party more than a week ago. You need to build a bridge and get over it already."

She slides her chair and music stand into the corner and flops across her bed. She stares at the ceiling without saying a word, probably hoping I'll give up if she doesn't respond. But this poor me attitude is getting ridiculous.

"So, you want to tell me what that Shane guy did?" I

put on my best sympathetic sister smile, determined not to roll my eyes or laugh if it turns out to be something silly like the time Anthony Matthews said he liked her new shirt, and she burst into tears right in the middle of band practice.

Laina crumples into a sobbing mess and collapses into her pillows. I sit down beside her and pat her back. I'm tempted to suggest that she cut back on the melodrama, but she's been super-sensitive for months, and I'm starting to wonder if Shane is just the tip of the iceberg.

She clutches Mr. Cuddles, the giant, white teddy bear that Jarod gave her for her birthday last year. "He kissed me," she whispers. "The day I gave him a ride home from school? Shane kissed me, and then he told me to pretend it never happened."

I clench my fists and fight the urge to punch something. Seriously, what is with these guys? It's no wonder Shane and Jarod used to be best friends. They're exactly alike!

I think of the way Jarod looked at me when I caught him staring during the movie, and while we were eating those ridiculously huge brownie sundaes. I remember the way he held me, the way his lips pressed against mine … and the way he's acted like nothing has changed between us ever since.

At least Jarod wasn't the first guy I've ever kissed. Laina's been saving her virgin lips for that perfect, fairy tale moment. She was waiting for Prince Charming to ride in on a white horse and declare his undying love for her, guaranteeing a perfect happily-ever-after.

It's got to be killing her that her first kiss was with some other girl's boyfriend.

"So now you're over him, right? Want me to kill him for you?"

Laina laughs through her tears and shakes her head. "I don't think that would help. Besides, it's not his fault." She buries her face in Mr. Cuddles' tummy and her whole body shakes with sobs.

I grab the teddy bear and pull it away from Laina's face. It takes every ounce of willpower I have not to rip it out of her hands and tear its stupid smiling head right off its shoulders. The only thing that stops me is knowing that I would have to explain myself. And I'm not quite ready to announce that I've lost control of my own love life.

I take a deep breath and unclench my jaw enough to speak. "Don't tell me you still *like* that creep!"

I'm such a hypocrite.

But I don't care. It's one thing to let someone as perfect as Jarod mess with my head, when I know we have a genuine connection, and he might eventually come around. It's another thing entirely for Laina, who could literally get any guy she wants, to allow a jerk like Shane to make her feel unimportant.

"But what if it's my fault?" Laina asks. "What if I'm a really, really bad kisser? What if he was going to dump Rachel for me, but then I kissed him and ruined everything?"

"I thought he kissed you."

"Well, I kissed him back." She buries her face in Mr. Cuddles' fur again and screams.

I grab the teddy bear from Laina and throw it across the room with as much force as I can manage. I smile when it hits the wall with a thump, and I imagine Jarod's head slamming against the wall on top of that white, fluffy, teddy bear body. Laina shakes her head and jumps up to retrieve Mr. Cuddles.

I resist the urge to throw him out the window.

"Okay, you have to tell me everything," I say. "Because we are totally not forgiving these guys—this guy—unless there's a heck of a lot more to the story. He'd better have a terrific reason for hurting us—you—or he's history!"

Laina grabs her diary from her nightstand and opens it to the entry for February fifteenth. She hands it to me with a tired smile. "Here, I wrote it all down. You can read it."

I grab the book from her hands and settle back into a pile of pillows propped up against the wall to read. Laina isn't kidding when she says she wrote it all down. She's always so afraid that she might say or do the wrong thing that she keeps a super-detailed record of her life. She actually re-reads the conversations later and analyzes everything about them.

The spiral notebook she hands me is worn and tattered, and already nearly full, even though a quick flip through the pages tells me she only started writing in this one eleven days ago.

I used to sneak into Laina's room to read her old diaries when she wasn't home, because she fills them up so fast that there is always a new "old diary" full of juicy gossip to read. But she came home early one day and caught me, and so Dad built her a wooden box with a giant padlock on it, and Mom let her put a lock on her bedroom door, as long as she promised to only lock the door for privacy when she wasn't home. Laina has never voluntarily let me read her diary before.

I take a deep breath and slowly exhale, fighting to hide my excitement. Not that I really care about Laina's first kiss. Knowing my sister, it was probably an innocent peck so insignificant that it wouldn't even count for anyone but her. She's not the type to get into a romance-novel-worthy make out session, but her perfectionist compulsions can create drama out of anything.

The diary might have useful information about Jarod, though. Obviously, he hasn't told her that he kissed me, because she would have said something by now, but maybe he's said something that can give me a clue. I'm way better at analyzing boy language than Laina is. All I need is a little hint. And she has full conversations transcribed here, ready to analyze.

"You realize I'll have to read everything since the kiss too, right?" I ask. "Otherwise, I might not get a fully accurate picture of the situation."

Laina nods glumly and flops back against her pillows, crying into Mr. Cuddles while I read.

I quickly skim through Laina's detailed account of her conversation with Shane, which led to not only one but *two* amazingly steamy kisses that made my mini make out session with Jarod on the porch look tame. But when it really started to heat up, she got scared that Shane might push her too far, and she pulled away.

He tried to apologize, but when he told her that she was "the most phenomenal girl" he had ever met, she assumed that he was only feeding her a lame pick-up line, and she made him get out of the car. His "we can pretend this never happened" sounds more like a desperate attempt to backtrack to a time when she wasn't angry with him than his way of trying to forget that he kissed her. And after our conversation last Saturday, I'm willing to bet that Shane is totally in lust with Laina.

Maybe even love.

But in-between detailed descriptions of those kisses and her tortured analysis of his supposed lack of feelings, Laina keeps referring to "the incident with Anthony Matthews." She compares Shane to Anthony and worries that Shane would have turned into "another Anthony" if she hadn't stopped him soon enough. But she doesn't explain "the incident" at all.

"What happened with Anthony Matthews?"

Laina shakes her head and refuses to look at me. "It's not important."

Liar.

I bite my lip and go back to reading, trying to piece together the puzzle with the few clues she's left behind. Because the thing that happened with Anthony is definitely important. And I'm afraid it's a much bigger deal than she wants me to believe.

The entries for the days immediately following the kiss are basically useless. Laina mentions witnessing a fight between Shane and Rachel on the morning of the sixteenth. Then, she rambles on for pages about how Shane has been alternately ignoring her and staring at her like some creepy stalker ever since.

There's almost nothing about Jarod, except for when she whines about how she can't confide in him about kissing Shane because the boys are still fighting and she doesn't even know what their fight is about.

Really? How can someone with a straight-A average since kindergarten be this stupid? I want to smack her with this book and tell her to wake up and make a choice already, because it isn't fair to Rachel and me for her to keep stringing both boys along.

I close the notebook and take a deep breath. There's nothing in here that explains Laina's overly melodramatic reaction to her first kiss. Nothing except the shiver-inducing cryptic comment scrawled at the bottom of the last entry. "Jarod warned me about guys like Anthony. He would be so disappointed if he knew I almost let it happen again." Maybe this isn't really about a kiss.

"What happened with Anthony?"

She glares at me. "Nothing."

"Oh, right, I already asked that, didn't I?" I may not be able to ask directly, but my ditzy little sister act is usually pretty effective when I want information. "So did anything else happen with Shane that day? Anything you forgot to write down?"

She shakes her head. "No, that's all. Every detail."

"He didn't ..." I hesitate. I'm not sure how to ask, without sounding like I'm talking to a two-year-old about Stranger Danger. "You just kissed, right? He didn't say or do anything else?"

"I wrote it all down." She sighs. "It's hopeless, isn't it?

We're never going to be together."
"You may be right, but not for the reasons you think."

Chapter Nine

Laina sits up. "What?"

I shake my head. "You are the most clueless person I know. Worse than any boy. Unless you're leaving out a major piece of the puzzle, it's obvious that Shane is totally in love with you. But you keep pushing him away. He's going to give up on you eventually, if you refuse to even give him a chance. No guy is going to keep hanging around, waiting for you forever."

Except for Jarod.

"But that kiss didn't actually mean anything. Kendra told me—"

"Kendra's a witch!"

Laina frowns. "She's not afraid to go after what she wants. That doesn't mean—"

"No. I don't care what the Witch said." Kendra is a parasite who gets her kicks out of destroying people. She wormed her way into Laina's life when someone (most likely

Kendra herself) started spreading particularly nasty rumors about Laina back in junior high. Kendra publicly accused Rachel and Marsa, Laina's two best friends, of spreading the rumors, and even though she didn't have a shred of evidence, everyone believed her. She's been slowly chipping away at Laina's self-esteem ever since.

"But what if—"

"She's wrong, and I can prove it." I flip open Laina's diary. She can't argue with her own record. "February fifteenth, Shane kisses you and calls you the most phenomenal girl he's ever met. Guys don't say things like that!"

She laughs and waves her hand dismissively. "Of course they do. Guys say crap like that all the time."

"Maybe they say things like that to *you*, because you *are* freaking phenomenal. But they don't say it to normal girls."

No, the rest of us get things like the phenomenal disappointment of being called by our perfect big sister's names mere seconds after the most amazing kisses of our entire lives. I can't decide if she's being intentionally dense to fish for compliments, or if she really doesn't know she has every guy in school salivating over her.

I flip through the pages of her journal, looking for some proof that will make her believe me. "February sixteenth, Rachel and Shane are fighting and Rachel storms off when she sees you. February seventeenth, Shane stares at you all through chemistry class, but won't talk to you. February eighteenth, he tries to steal and read your diary."

I look up. "Hello? Duh! He's secretly in love with you and he can't figure out what you want from him, so he's desperately trying to figure it out." I shrug. "Okay, so he conveniently forgot to break up with his current girlfriend before making out with you, but I think he has real feelings for you. Maybe you should give him a chance."

"But none of that really means anything," Laina insists. "Shane and Rachel have been fighting practically since they started dating. That's what insanely popular people do. And maybe Shane was staring because I had spinach in my teeth or something. And every guy I know tries to steal my diary. Shane's just jumping on the bandwagon."

I toss the diary aside and pull out my sure-fire weapon. "Then explain to me why Emily told me at lunch today that Rachel thinks her boyfriend is in love with you."

Laina grimaces. "Emily loves spreading rumors, even if she has to make them up herself. You saw her campaign for Snow Queen. You know you can't believe a word she says."

I bite my lip. Clearly, I need a different approach.

"Well, even if Shane didn't already want you, which he does even if you don't believe me, he will by the time we're through." I grin. "You know how guys are all super competitive? All you have to do is get a boyfriend. As soon as you're not available anymore, Shane will wake up and see what he's been missing, and he'll totally come running."

"Yeah, right. I'm not you, remember? I don't want to hook up with the first guy to smile at me. Where am I supposed to find this amazing boyfriend in the first place?"

Luckily, she has her face buried in Mr. Cuddles' tummy again, so she doesn't see the tear running down my cheek. She's right. She's not like me. She actually has a chance with the most perfect guy who ever lived, and Jarod will only ever see me as her little sister.

She looks up and studies my face. "What did you say about Jarod?"

Oops. I must have said that out loud. And now I have to say something quick or admit that I'm in love with her biggest fan.

"Why not Jarod?" I ask, slipping on my cheerful, carefree voice. "He's super-hot and totally sweet. I'd date him in a heartbeat, if he wanted me. You guys are always together anyway. Let him be your boyfriend." Between my superior acting skills and Laina's cluelessness, I totally pull off the I'm-not-in-love-with-your-best-friend charade.

She scoffs. "It's not like I can wave my magic wand and make him want me."

I point at Mr. Cuddles. "You don't need a magic wand. Jarod's totally in love with you."

Laina laughs and sets the teddy bear aside. "So now I have two hot boys who are secretly in love with me? Come on, Andi, this is real life, not some silly fairy tale."

I fold my arms and take a slow, deep breath, stifling the urge to seriously injure my poor, pathetic, perfect-yet-utterly-clueless, big sister.

"No, you don't have two boys who are secretly in love with you."

Her eyes widen and I realize I'm letting my emotions show again. I swallow and slip back into my carefree tone. "You have one boy, Shane, who is secretly in love with you, and one boy, Jarod, who tells you that he loves you every single day, but you totally blow him off. And yes, they're both hot."

She laughs. "Whatever you say, little sister. Who am I to spoil your crazy delusions?"

I give up.

There's no way I'm going to convince her. I need a new strategy.

Again.

I jump up with an excited squeal. "Oh my Gollum, Laina, you know what we need?"

She blinks and then stares at me, her eyes wide with shock. I bounce up and down a few times for good measure to emphasize my "excitement."

"Remember when we were little and we used to play with Barbie dolls and go to the carnival, and we never even cared about what anyone else thought, because boys were yucky anyway, and we didn't have to worry about trying to impress anyone?" I grab her hands and pull her off the bed. I continue bouncing until she's grinning and bouncing right along with me. "Let's do that again!"

She stops bouncing and arches one eyebrow. "You want to play with Barbie?"

I laugh. "I don't need a Barbie doll. I live with the real-life version, remember?" I nudge her and she pushes me away. She hates the nickname, but that doesn't make it any less true. "Tomorrow night. Let's go out and have a totally crazy, girls-only night, where we pretend that guys are still yucky, cooties and all, and we don't even care about what they think of us. We'll be totally wild and get in all sorts of crazy trouble."

Laina nods slowly. "As long as we don't get too wild. You can't get me grounded."

"Don't worry. It will all be Laina-approved fun. No actual reputations will be harmed in the making of this girls' night." I sit at her desk and pull out a sheet of paper. "All we need is a plan!"

This has to work, because I'm totally out of new strategies, and the only thing worse than a perfect sister is a depressed Barbie doll.

I write out a quick script for a night full of random silliness and clever word play that I know she'll appreciate, and I show my "plan" to Laina. As soon as I have her approval on it, I hurry to my room, grabbing the phone and Mom's laptop on my way. It's time to turn this gibberish and nonsense into a real plan, and Shane Crawford is going to help me to do it. If all goes well tomorrow night, Laina and Shane will get together, she'll be happy again, and Jarod will be free to pursue other interests. Like me.

Shane answers his phone halfway through the first ring. "Alaina?" I can practically hear his heart pounding through the phone. He clears his throat and takes a deep breath. "I was just thinking about you," he says in a soft, gravelly voice that makes even my heart skip a beat.

"Nope. Try again, lover boy."

His disappointment resonates through the thick silence.

"Oh. It's her obnoxious social secretary, right? Listen, you don't have to worry. I haven't tried to talk to her. I'm working on something big."

"If you want to show Laina that you're really sorry, I'm going to give you the perfect opportunity. Tomorrow night."

Shane lets loose a long string of profanity, and I hear something crash on his side of the line. I'm tempted to hang up on him, but this is too important. I finally have to push all of the buttons of the phone at once to catch his attention with a loud beep in his ear.

"Um, Shane?" I say when his little temper tantrum finally winds down. "Yeah, that's not really going to work in your favor. Laina has this thing about swearing, and she's not going to hang around for long if you can't control your mouth." I sigh. "If seeing Laina tomorrow night is too much for you to handle, then we can forget this whole thing. You're on your own."

"No, don't hang up!" He takes a deep breath. "I want to talk to her. I do. But I have to work tomorrow night and I kind of need the hours."

"That's perfect." I grab a pencil and a blank sheet of paper, and then I pull the page of random gibberish out of my pocket. "Where do you work, and when?" My plan is generic enough to fit him into the narrative somewhere.

"I'm working the closing shift at Burger Barn. From five to eleven. I should get a dinner break at seven-thirty, unless we're still slammed with the Saturday night dinner crowd, in which case I won't get my break until eight."

"I don't need a play-by-play of your entire night, lover boy. I only need to know the least crowded time for a Saturday night at Burger Barn."

"I don't know. Right before closing, I guess. About ten-thirty, maybe?"

"Okay, tomorrow night, I'm taking Laina out for a girls' night. At about ten-thirty, we'll stop by for a snack. It has to look totally random, so you'd better be working and not conveniently on break when we show up. Got it?"

"Okay. Then what?"

"Then you talk to her. You're working the register, right? So take your time filling our order. You have Laina as a captive audience for as long as you can stretch it out. It shouldn't be that hard. Figure out what you want to say, and find a way to say it without looking like a complete idiot."

"Okay."

"And Shane?"

"Yeah?"

"Lose the girlfriend."

"Right."

I hang up and study the script for tomorrow night's adventure. Chatting with Shane while he's supposed to be working could totally count as the last item on my list, when we're supposed to "harass the employees of local businesses." Now, I just have to fill the rest of our "crime spree" with innocent mischief.

By the time Laina appears to tell me that dinner's ready, I've slapped together an English paper that should earn me at least a B-minus, and I have the perfect plan for our girls' night out. And I don't even have to feel guilty about manipulating Laina this time. She would totally thank me if she knew what I'm doing for her.

Chapter Ten

"So what are we doing?" Laina asks as I dig through her closet, searching for an appropriate outfit.

I hand her the script of random gibberish that I composed last night. As if I'm going to tell her the real plan.

"Why can't I wear this?" she asks. "If we don't care what anyone else thinks about us tonight, why does it even matter what I wear?"

"Because there's no way you can really feel good about the way you look if you're hiding behind those gross clothes."

There's no way Laina's going to meet Shane looking like she picked her outfit from her clothing drive's reject pile. I'm constantly buying things that actually fit her body, but whatever she can't return gets shoved to the back of her closet, price tags still attached. It's like she's afraid to be noticed. I've blamed Kendra's toxic comments for whittling away at Laina's self-image, but maybe the "Anthony Matthews incident" has something to do with it. I have to find out what happened.

"Here." I toss Laina a black leather miniskirt and a red V-neck sweater that hugs her curves perfectly. "Put these on."

She yanks off her t-shirt and throws it into a pile of dirty clothes next to her bed, then slips the sweater over her head and pulls it over her perfectly flat stomach. But she kicks the miniskirt across the room to another, larger, pile of dirty clothes in the corner. "There's no way I'm wearing that," she says. "Even if it wasn't freezing outside, you have a better chance of convincing birds to fly north for the winter than you'll ever have of convincing me to wear that thing. I don't know what possessed you to buy it in the first place."

I sigh. "Fine. But will you at least wear these instead?" I hold up a pair of black skinny jeans and the cute, black ballet flats that I found on sale last weekend.

She nods and slips them on quickly, and I retrieve the miniskirt to hang back in her closet. This was the best fifty bucks I ever spent. All I have to do is pull it out of the closet, and Laina doesn't even fight me on the "second choice" outfit I select for her.

First up for our night of crime, we have to "Rob the mall."

Rob works at the information desk on Saturday nights, and I thought we could stop by to get in some flirting practice and a quick ego boost.

The look on Laina's face, when I toss her a black ski mask and tell her to drive to the mall for the first phase of our night, is totally priceless. She holds the mask between her thumb and forefinger and shoots me a you've-got-to-be-kidding look.

"Are you ready?" I open the passenger door and climb into her car. It's too bad I completely bombed my driving test. Tonight would be more fun if I could kidnap her and drag her along, without the need to convince her to go along with my plan. But Mom won't let me try for my license again until I pass driver's ed.

Laina stands on the sidewalk, arms folded and keys firmly clenched in her fist. I open the door again and shake my head at her. "Will you relax? I'm not about to get us arrested or anything. Besides, do you really think I'd let you wear that mask after all the time I spent on your hair and makeup? Please."

She shakes her head, and then nods and gets into the car. "Where are we really going?" she asks as she starts the engine.

Once I finally convince her that we are actually going to the mall, where she won't have to do anything even the tiniest bit illegal, she eases her car into gear, and we drive across town. She peppers me with questions, trying to make me spill the real details of my plan, but I'm the queen of evasion.

She should know I'd never let my secrets slip.

When we walk into the mall and I head straight to the information booth, her eyes widen and she pulls me back outside. "I knew you couldn't go a whole night without flirting with boys." She laughs. "But can we make this a short stop? Rob's kind of arrogant. I can only take so much of him before I want to tear my own hair out."

"What? Rob's a sweetheart. I think you're confusing him with Josh." I grin at her, and when she finally relents, I saunter over to the information booth and flash my most brilliant smile, with Laina following right on my heels.

Rob grins and leans across the desk. He's practically drooling already, and I haven't even said a word. This is too easy.

"What can I do for you lovely ladies tonight?" Rob

asks.

"We need some information. This is the place for it, correct?" I point to the giant "Information" sign hanging above his head.

"Of course." He stands up and straightens his tie, and then he looks at Laina. "I'm the man with all the answers. I'm always happy to help you, Alaina." He glances at me. "And your little sister, right?"

Seriously? I know we don't exactly hang out together, but I've spent enough time with Laina and Jarod and his friends that you'd think he could at least remember my name.

I flash my sexiest smile, the one that never fails to get a reaction from boys, and lean on the desk. "Really? All the answers?" I arch one eyebrow. "I'll bet we can stump you."

"I'll take that bet." He grins at Laina. "If you can ask even one question that I don't know the answer to, I'll leave your diary alone for a week. But if you can't, you owe me lunch."

Laina's eyes light up. She's always afraid guys are trying to steal her super-secret diary, so his terms must be too good to pass up. "It's a deal."

And just like that, I'm officially not even a part of this conversation anymore. Laina throws random questions at him, one after another. "Who invented the zipper?" "What classic author used to write under the pen name Peter Jackson?" "What's the atomic weight of ..." I don't know. Some random element that I've never even heard of.

Rob sounds like a robot with a Wikipedia-like answer for every single question. He could totally be making it all up, but Laina seems to be satisfied, so I guess he knows what he's talking about.

I try to force my way back into the conversation, but Rob only answers my questions with short, one or two-word responses before returning his full attention to Laina. When his boss comes stomping over and orders us to leave so that

Rob can get back to work, it's not exactly a devastating blow.

There aren't any long lines of people waiting for answers to pressing mall questions, and any other time, I probably would have argued our right to hang out wherever we wanted to, but I'm beyond ready to leave.

Phase one of our "crime spree" is a bust.

"I hate being your little sister," I say as we walk away.

"What? Why?"

I roll my eyes. "Do you always have to be the center of attention?"

"But you're the one Rob was being nice to. He made fun of every single thing I said."

We reach the car, and I yank open the door, but I don't get in. I spin around to face her. "How can you not know that Rob was trying to flirt with you?" I totally deserve a medal for the way I manage to keep my voice calm, even though Miss Perfect is so freaking annoying.

"What? No. That's not flirting. That's insulting my intelligence. He's been trying to prove that he's smarter than me ever since I kicked his butt in the sixth grade spelling bee."

Total face palm moment.

"Laina, he's trying to show off. Yeah, he's not very good at the whole flirting thing, but in his own socially awkward way, Rob's trying to get your attention. He totally wants you."

"Yeah, right," she scoffs. "Every boy in school is secretly in love with me and they're all way too shy to say anything to me directly, right?"

"Yes."

"Whatever. Forgive me if I have a hard time believing that one, but I've noticed that all of these 'terminally shy' boys never have the slightest bit of trouble when they want to ask you out. Or anyone else. You seriously want me to believe that all of these confident, cocky, and even flat-out arrogant boys suddenly lose their cool and can't express their true feelings when I'm around, because they're too into me? How does that make sense?"

I laugh. "Do you even know how intimidating you are? Sometimes, I'm even afraid to talk to you, and I'm not in love with you."

Laina shoves me into the car. Then, she walks around to the driver's side and climbs in herself. "I know you're trying to cheer me up and all, but cut the crap, okay? Enough with the cheesy pep talk. You can only stretch the truth so far before it completely breaks down on you." She starts the car. "You said that we had three phases to complete tonight. That was phase one, right? So what's phase two?"

I push Rob out of my mind and turn my focus back to the night's plan. After all, if this works, by the time we go home tonight, Laina and Shane will be together and maybe Jarod will finally be ready to move on.

I so don't need Rob.

Chapter Eleven

"We're going drinking and driving," I say. "Let's go get some beer."

Laina pulls out of the parking lot and drives past three liquor stores and directly to the grocery store down the street. "I assume you're talking about root beer, correct?" she says, as she pulls into a parking space.

"Of course. Let's get high on life, big sister!"

"Um, I think alcohol is technically a depressant. So you don't actually get high on beer."

I giggle. "Laina, you think too much. Come on. Let's go get our beer and show the world that the Andersen sisters know how to party right on a Saturday night." I hop out of the car and do a perfect cartwheel in the parking lot. Then, I jump up and run for the door. "Race you!"

Laina opts for diet ginger ale, because she doesn't really like root beer, and "ale is just as appropriate as beer for drinking and driving." By the time we pay for our sodas, we're laughing so hard that I swear the cashier thinks we're already drunk.

When we walk back to the parking lot, Laina turns to say something to me, and she walks straight into Dave, who is trying to get past us into the store. He grabs her arm to steady her. "What's so funny?"

"Oh, we're a little bit drunk." Laina giggles. "Or, at least, we're getting there."

Dave raises one eyebrow. "Alaina Andersen is drunk? How did that happen?"

I roll my eyes. No matter how much I hate living in Laina's perfect shadow, I can't let a stupid misunderstanding ruin her pristine reputation. "Not really. It's a sister thing."

Laina holds up the plastic bag with our sodas inside. "See?" she giggles. "We're getting ready to go drinking and driving now." And then she explains our girls' night crime spree to him.

Dave's eyes widen, and he smiles. He drapes an arm around her shoulders and leans in to whisper, "Can I come, too? I haven't been drinking and driving in almost a week."

"Sorry. No boys allowed." I grab Laina's arm and steer her toward the car before Dave can start drooling. He's never even looked twice at her before, so why is he suddenly acting like I don't even exist? I'm so not in the mood for a repeat of what happened at the mall.

Laina giggles. "Why not? The more the merrier, right? Besides, you made me suffer through that whole thing with Rob." She twists out of my grasp and grins at Dave, handing him her bottle of ginger ale.

Dave takes a swig of the soda and follows us across the parking lot. I climb into Laina's car and shake my head. "I already told you, this is a sister thing. We don't have room for you."

Laina hops into the driver's seat and rolls down her window to wave at Dave. "Catch us if you can," she yells, before pulling out of the parking lot.

We have a little over two hours to kill before I'm supposed to deliver Laina to Shane at the Burger Barn, and randomly driving around town gets boring really fast. I'd expected to take a lot more time working on phase one, and I didn't even think to build in a backup plan. So as irritating as he can be at times, I'm not terribly annoyed when Dave decides to crash our narrative.

At least it adds something to the monotony of drinking and driving.

"Oh look." I point at Dave's headlights in the rearview mirror. "We're leading a high speed chase through the crowded city streets."

Laina smirks. "I don't know if twenty-five miles an hour when we're the only two cars on the road really qualifies."

"What are you talking about? I saw three other cars less than two minutes ago, which is probably more traffic than this street usually sees on a Saturday night, and twenty-five miles an hour is like light speed to a turtle."

"Well, in that case, we need a good chase scene soundtrack." She turns the radio to the only good, non-country station in town and cranks the volume up as high as it will go, which isn't really very high because her ancient car still has the original, crappy 1970s stereo system, eight-track player and all. But we sing along anyway.

I manage to drag out phase two of our plan by repeatedly guzzling my soda and then insisting that we need to stop at another grocery store for more beer. Dave is right behind us every single time we stop, and by the third "beer run," I nearly forget that Dave wasn't supposed to be part of our adventure.

When ten o'clock finally rolls around, I declare the drinking and driving portion of our evening officially finished. We pull back into the parking lot of the first grocery store, and Dave announces that we need a reward for successfully pulling off our crime without getting caught. He runs in and returns a moment later with three giant candy bars.

"You guys are nuts." He tears open his candy bar and takes a humongous bite, and then he grins through a mouthful of chocolate before tossing one of the candy bars to each of us. Laina fumbles and drops hers, but I snatch mine out of the air, ripping it open and taking a huge bite all in one smooth move. I smile as if it's no big deal, even though I could never do it again if I practiced for a million years.

Dave grins. "That's impressive."

"Yeah, well, that's me. Impressive."

"You got that right." He takes a step closer, and his eyes glint in the moonlight.

Yeah, I've still got it.

"What's next?" Laina asks. "On to phase three?"

"Phase three?" Dave asks. "What's that?"

"Oh, our night is only beginning," I say. "Laina's little miss innocent act is the perfect cover. No one ever suspects that the Andersen sisters are such dangerous criminals."

Dave takes another huge bite of his candy bar. "It's always the quiet ones that you have to worry about."

"Oh, yeah. Don't let these pretty faces fool you. We're trouble." I glance at my watch. "It's ten-fifteen now. We'd better get moving, or we're totally going to miss our chance to pull off phase three before curfew."

Laina giggles. "Do criminal masterminds worry about curfew? That kind of ruins our dangerous image, don't you think, Dave?"

He inhales sharply, nearly choking on a mouthful of chocolate. "Ten-fifteen?" He tosses the rest of his candy bar into the trash can next to the supermarket door, hugs Laina and smiles sheepishly at me. "I've gotta go. I was supposed to pick Heather up from work at nine, and she's gonna kill me."

He races off. "I'll see you later. If I'm still alive!"

"I thought Dave and Heather broke up last month," Laina says.

"I didn't even know they were together." I swallow the last, unappetizing bite of my candy bar. I don't care who he dates. I'm glad he has a girlfriend. This night is about one thing, and one thing only: getting Laina and Shane together so I can have Jarod. And maybe Dave should pay more attention to his girlfriend and quit following me around like a little, lost puppy.

"Come on," I say. "On to phase three!"

Shane looks up from the register as we walk into the Burger Barn, and his eyes widen when he sees Laina. For once, I'm glad she's so incredibly clueless, because it's beyond obvious that Shane's been waiting for us. If he was a dog, he'd be wagging his tail and jumping up on her right now. I catch his eye and shake my head slightly. He blushes and grabs a rag to wipe at the counter. This "random" meeting is totally not going to work if lover boy lets Laina know we planned it.

He turns his attention back to the couple studying the menu at the counter, and I exhale slowly. He's still watching Laina out of the corner of his eye, but it's not quite so obvious now.

Laina digs her fingernails into my arm and drags me into the ladies' room. "Did you know Shane was working tonight?"

Crap! I knew he was going to blow it.

I pull a tube of lip gloss out of my purse. "Paranoid much?" I turn toward the mirror and concentrate on touching up my lips before I turn back to look at her. "I'm not the one that's obsessed with that Shane guy. Maybe I should have called him to coordinate our schedules?"

She glares and taps her foot. "Did you plan it?"

"Right. I definitely planned this. Because I'm totally devious." I push my lower lip out in a classic pout. "You think I wanted to spend the rest of my night hiding in the bathroom? Hello? I'm your sister. I know how crazy-paranoid you are. Would I torture you on purpose?"

She shakes her head.

I pass her the tube of lip gloss. "Come on. I think he saw us when we came in. Let's show him what he's missing."

"What? No! I can't go out there. We have to leave."

"Not a chance. We're not supposed to care about what guys think of us, right?"

Laina snorts. "For a 'boy free' night, it's been pretty high on testosterone."

"I'm not the one who invited Dave to follow us around town." I reach for the door. "And I'm hungry. Let's get some food."

Laina leans against the door, so I can't pull it open. "We can hit the drive-thru on our way home, and I'll buy you anything you want. But I'm super tired. Let's leave."

"So you're gonna let him get away with it? You're not even going to torture him a little, tiny bit to make him pay?"

She hesitates. "How would you feel if the boy you've been secretly in love with for years finally kissed you, and it didn't even mean anything to him? It's humiliating."

I grab her shoulders and shake her a little too hard. "He wanted you to pretend that the kiss never even happened, right?"

She nods.

"So start pretending. Let's go out there and act like he doesn't even matter. He needs to know that the kiss meant less than nothing to you. You're strong. You don't need him.

You have lots of other options, and if Jar—if Shane wants you, he'll have to prove he's worthy."

I swipe a fresh coat of gloss across her lips and arrange her long, blonde curls for the maximum wow effect. Then I push her out of the bathroom, and we saunter up to the counter.

Well, I saunter.

Laina kind of shuffles along behind me in an I-wish-this-floor-would-open-up-and-swallow-me-right-now kind of way. But at least she doesn't run to the car.

The restaurant is completely empty now, so we have Shane's undivided attention.

Perfect.

"We'll take two large cups of ice water. To go, please." Laina's voice cracks and breaks, but at least she looks him in the eye when she says it.

"Actually," I say, "make that two cheeseburgers and a large order of fries. And we'll eat it here."

Laina looks at me, her eyes wide. "What are you *doing*?" she mouths. I smile and raise one eyebrow. I didn't go through all this hassle tonight to let her ruin it now.

She takes a step backward, and I can tell she's thinking about running away. But there's no way I'm going to let her leave until we get what we came for.

And I'm not talking about the cheeseburgers.

Chapter Twelve

I giggle. "We're kind of hungry. Breaking the law works up an appetite, you know."

Laina laughs when Shane's eyes widen, and I can tell she's remembering Dave's reaction when she accidentally convinced him that she was drunk. "Oh yeah, we're nothing but trouble," she says, grinning at me. "You know, come to think of it, I am hungry. A cheeseburger sounds good." She looks at Shane and her smile falters. "But we'll take that to go."

"Are you sure you can't stay?" Shane waves his hand at the empty restaurant. "I think I could probably get you a seat at our very finest table." He reaches across the counter to take Laina's hand, but pulls back when she flinches. "I'll do anything you need."

She cocks her head to one side, eyeing him curiously, and he blushes.

"I mean, well, that's the Burger Barn promise. We

guarantee that your Burger Barn dining experience will be ... I'm supposed to make your night special."

"Thanks, but we're kind of in a hurry. We still have crimes to commit. Right, Andi? Phase three? So we'll take that food to go."

"Actually," I say, "this is our last stop. After this, we're going home to bed." I pull the gibberish version of our plan from my purse and pass it to her. We're here to "harass the employees of local businesses," which means she has to stay. And she has to talk to Shane.

"Next stop is your bed, huh?" Shane asks. "Need any help with that?"

All the color drains from Laina's face. Her eyes widen and she takes a step back. In her panic-stricken eyes, I see a reflection of the same terror she described in her diary.

I want to reach over the counter and slap Shane. Hard. He was supposed to be apologizing for hurting Laina, not driving her away. Why does he think I gave him time to plan his approach?

I grab Laina's hand to keep her from bolting, and then I shoot a glare at Shane, hoping he's not too dense to realize that he's about to crash and burn. "We'll just take our food please."

"Oh, of course." Shane's finger hovers for a moment over the cash register, but then he drops his hand to his side. "I forgot. What did you want?"

I'll give him some credit, at least. He's doing a pretty good job of delaying our order. Not that it will do him much good, if he doesn't stop with the creeptastic remarks, but at least he got part of my instructions right.

"Two large ice waters, please," Laina squeaks.

I nudge her with my elbow.

"Oh yeah, and two cheeseburgers. To go."

"We'll eat here," I say. "And don't forget my fries. I'm hungry."

Shane pushes a few buttons, and then he looks up again. "Do you want fries with that?"

I roll my eyes.

"Oh yeah." He blushes. "You already said that." He pushes another button, and then he smiles at Laina. "So what have you been up to tonight?"

I wait for Laina to answer, but she's still looking around wildly, as if she's trying to plan an escape route. And I kind of don't blame her, but she's never going to get over this thing with Shane if she doesn't talk to him.

Pushing her forward, I start in on a detailed explanation of our crime spree in my most carefree, bubbly voice. I choose my words carefully to make it all sound much more wild and exciting than it actually was, hoping to bring back the Laina who didn't care about what people were thinking, and had no problem with announcing to the world, or at least to Dave, that she was drunk.

By the time I finish the story, Laina's lost that scared little bunny rabbit look, and she's laughing. "Yeah, we're a couple of dangerous criminals."

Shane snickers. "How would you like to add grand theft auto to your list of felonies?"

"Ooh, does this mean you're gonna let us take your car?" Laina asks. Her eyes light up and I resist the urge to make a sarcastic remark about his beat-up old clunker. It's even older than Laina's heap. He could probably leave it unlocked and running, keys in the ignition, and still no one would try to take it. But for some reason, Laina loves it. Maybe it's because it's a convertible. Or maybe it reminds her of those cheesy old movies from the fifties that she likes to watch so much.

Or maybe because it belongs to Shane.

He laughs and shakes his head. "Sorry. You know I don't let anybody drive my baby. But I'll give you a ride in her." He hesitates, and then he takes a deep breath and reaches across the counter to brush a stray curl out of Laina's eyes. He tucks it behind her ear and rests his palm against her cheek for a moment before pulling away again. "Anywhere you want to go."

I feel like I'm intruding on a private moment, but she's still freaking out. If I tried to give them some privacy now, he'd lose her for sure.

Laina closes her eyes and sighs dreamily, and I relax a little bit.

I wonder if Shane is going to try to kiss her right here and now. I wonder if she'll let him. But then she shudders and opens her eyes. I can tell she's still struggling with the urge to flee, and I tense up, ready to grab her arm and drag her back if I have to, but she plasters on a smile and forces a small, tight laugh.

"Anywhere I want?" She hesitates. "What about Disneyland? I've always wanted to go there, and they say it's the happiest place on earth."

I snort. Disneyland? My sister might be good at practically everything, but she sucks at improvisation.

Shane grins. "Sure. Want to go tonight? My shift here ends in about an hour, and then I'm all yours. I might even be able to find a deserted dirt road where we could run out of gas along the way, and then I can really take you to the happiest place on earth."

He winks at her and I gasp. The guy's a freaking moron! Did he not see her reaction earlier?

The color drains from Laina's face, but she doesn't try to escape. She stands there, speechless, while Shane grins at her. It's like watching a train wreck in slow motion. I can see the disaster coming, but I can't do anything to stop it.

Laina takes a slow, deep breath. "Well, if I can't steal your car, then how does grand theft auto fit into our plan? You do realize that I'm not up to committing any real felonies, right?"

"Yeah, I got that." Shane flashes a smile so sexy that even my heart skips a beat, and then he reaches across the counter to take her hand. "Don't worry. Leading you down the path to a life of crime is not exactly the way I'd like to corrupt you."

And just like that, he's blown it again.

Laina turns a brilliant shade of fire engine red, and she backs away from the counter, pulling out of my grasp. She looks like she wants to run, but I think she's afraid he might pounce if she takes her eyes off of him for even a moment.

I've gotta give the boy credit. He certainly isn't shy.

Incredibly stupid, but not shy.

I know I should probably step up and save them from this hole they're digging themselves into, but the train-wreck is too ridiculous. My giggles turn into full-on laughter, and before I know it, I'm laughing too hard to even stand up straight. I slide to the floor and lean back against the counter.

"That's not what I meant," Laina mumbles.

"Oh, I know," he says. "You're not like that. That's what I love about you. Don't mind me, I'm ... I don't know why I said that."

Even from my position on the floor, I can see the panic growing in Laina's eyes. She's half a heartbeat away from running straight to Jarod's overprotective arms. Which is exactly the opposite of what should be happening.

"So how much do we owe you?" I ask, jumping to my feet, my laughter dissolving as I fight down a mini panic attack of my own.

Shane blinks rapidly, as if he's waking up from a dream. "What?"

I point to the cash register. "Our cheeseburgers and fries. How much?"

"Oh, right." He pushes a few buttons and then looks up again. "No charge. How can it be grand theft, if you pay for it?" He reaches behind the counter and grabs a little, plastic toy car, one of the Burger Barn kids' meal toys, and holds it up proudly. "And here. This makes it 'grand theft auto,' right?" He holds the car out toward Laina, but his cocky grin fades when she refuses to take it.

"We're gonna go sit down," I say, grabbing the car and pulling Laina toward an empty booth. "You'll bring that out to us when it's ready?"

"You wait for the food," Laina says. "I'll be right back." She twists her arm out of my grasp and bolts for the bathroom. I consider following her, but at this point, I think I'd only make it worse. Operation crime spree has been a complete and total bust from start to finish.

When did I lose control?

I slump into the booth and bury my face in my hands.

"I screwed up, didn't I?"

I look up to see Shane, standing next to me, staring across the room at the closed bathroom door.

"Yeah. Didn't I tell you to practice what you were going to say? What on earth possessed you to channel a drunken frat boy?"

He shoves his hands in his pockets and stares at the floor. "I know. I'm stupid. It's just … I don't know. I can't think straight when I'm around her. I practiced. Honest." He glances back toward the bathroom. "But as soon as I saw you guys walk in, my mind went blank."

He drops to his knees, hands clasped in supplication. "You can fix it, right? Let her know I'm not really a creep?"

"I don't know, lover boy. From what I've seen, I'm not too impressed. And Laina deserves to be with one of the good guys."

"Yeah." He stands slowly and backs away. "I know. I don't deserve her. Tell her I'm sorry, okay? I'd take it all back if I could. I didn't mean to … I'm sorry." He shuffles back to his place behind the counter and busies himself refilling straw dispensers and napkin holders, watching for Laina the entire time.

At least he has enough good sense to realize that he's blown it.

"Okay, I totally get why you like this Shane guy," I whisper, when Laina finally comes out of the bathroom. "I would definitely fall for a guy who looked at me the way he looks at you."

Laina shakes her head. "He's not interested in the real me."

I glance over my shoulder to where Shane is putting together our order. "That guy is completely in love with you."

"I cannot face him again. Maybe I could transfer to a different chemistry class. But the only other section is second period. That conflicts with band. Maybe there's an online option?"

"You're not gonna change your schedule," I say. "Don't be such a drama queen."

Shane brings over a tray with our cheeseburgers, and a mountain of fries. "Here's your 'grand theft' order. Let me know if you need anything else." He stares into Laina's eyes as he sets the tray down in front of her. "Whatever it takes to make you happy."

I don't think he's talking about the Burger Barn promise.

Laina nods, but she doesn't say anything. She looks at the table and starts rearranging the fries into random patterns on the tray. Finally, Shane clears his throat and smiles. "Well, if you want me, you know where to find me." He reaches out, as if to take Laina's hand again, but then he shakes his head, smiles at us, and returns to his station behind the cash register.

"See? He totally wants you."

Laina rolls her eyes. "Physical attraction isn't the same thing as love. Shane's a big flirt, but that's all it is. He has a girlfriend remember? What guy in his right mind would break up with the beautiful, perfect, head cheerleader for a band geek like me?"

"What guy in his right mind wouldn't?"

"But he's with Rachel."

"The way he's looking at you, I bet they're not even together anymore." At least, I hope they're not. I forgot to make sure they actually broke up. "Want me to go ask?"

I start to get up, but Laina grabs my arm and pulls me back to my seat. "Don't say a word," she hisses.

I polish off the fries and both burgers because Laina refuses to eat, and I was so not kidding when I said I was hungry. Laina fidgets nervously in her seat as I scarf down the food, staring at Shane the entire time. But she refuses to go talk to him, and he doesn't come back.

Finally, I can't think of any more reason to hang around, so I grab my purse and stand up. "You ready to go, then?"

Laina nods and jumps up, grabbing the empty tray and dumping it into the trash can next to our table.

"You sure you don't want me to talk to him? I'll find out everything you need to know."

"No!" Her protest obviously comes out louder than she'd intended, and she blushes when Shane looks up from the spot on the counter that he's been washing for the past five minutes. "I'll talk to him later, I promise." And she pulls me outside before I can object.

She won't, of course, but I will.

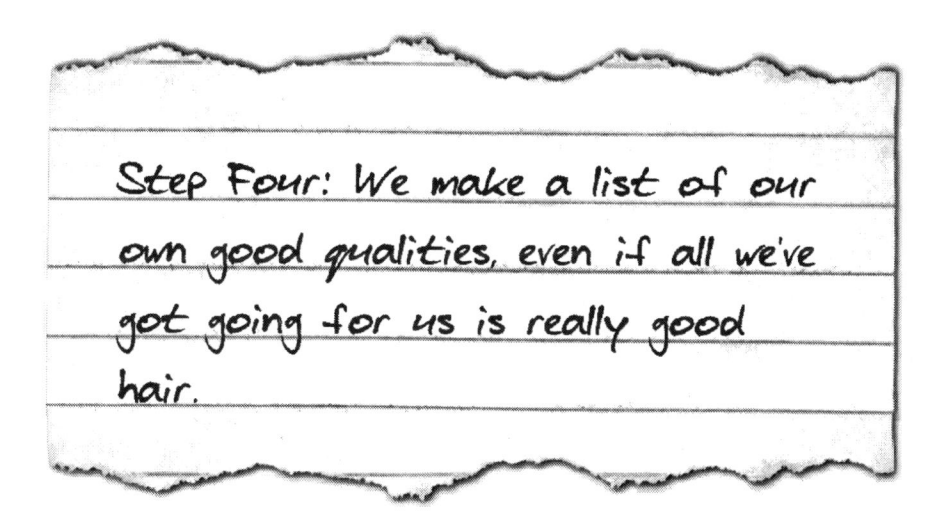

Step Four: We make a list of our own good qualities, even if all we've got going for us is really good hair.

Chapter Thirteen

I know I technically promised Jarod I'd help him get Laina, but that was before he kissed me. He can't expect me to keep the promise now. And watching Shane and Laina last night convinced me that they're kind of awkwardly perfect for each other.

At least, this is what I tell myself as I dial Shane's number.

Again, he answers on the first ring, all out of breath and excited. "Alaina? Hi. I wanted to call you, but I—"

"Wrong again."

"Oh. What do you want? I already know I was an idiot last night, so you can save your breath." He inhales sharply. "Wait. Did Alaina ask you to call? What did she say?"

"No, actually, she asked me not to call, but I need to make sure you're not going to break my sister's heart again. If you're still with Rachel …"

"What? No, of course not. That's over. I told you I was

going to break up with her." He pauses and takes a slow, deep breath. "But it turns out, I didn't even have to. Rachel sent me a text yesterday morning. She met someone else. So it's over and no one had to get hurt."

I can hear the smile behind his words, and I know he's proud of himself. "Lover boy, you're an idiot. You were supposed to break up with Rachel, not the other way around."

"What's the difference? As long as it's over, who cares who ended it? The point is that we're not together anymore, right?"

Why are boys so stupid about relationships?

"If you broke up with Rachel for Laina, then everyone would know you made your choice. But since you waited until Rachel dumped you for another guy, everyone will wonder if Laina's a rebound girl to get back at Rachel." I pause to let my words sink in. "And by 'everyone,' I mean Laina," I say, in case he's too dense to figure it out on his own.

"I didn't think about that."

"Yeah, you don't spend a lot of time thinking things through before you make stupid mistakes, do you?"

"If I was better at thinking things through, then I wouldn't make the stupid mistakes, now would I?" He sighs. "Okay, how do I fix it?"

"Find a way to make sure Laina knows you would have chosen her even if Rachel hadn't dumped your butt. And do it soon, because I wasted a perfectly good Saturday night on you."

I hang up and toss the phone aside.

I only have ten minutes left to get ready for church before Mom and Laina start pounding on my bedroom door. Luckily, I showered last night and braided my wet hair before I went to bed. All I have to do is throw on a dress, take out my braid and run a comb through my now-wavy hair. A touch of lip gloss gives me just the right sparkle to my yes-I'm-naturally-this-beautiful look. Eight and a half minutes later,

I'm ready to go and waiting by the front door.

Jarod is waiting when we walk into the church. He shakes hands with my parents and hugs Laina, and as they walk into the chapel, he grabs my hand. "Can we talk? It's important."

I shake my head. "Mom will shoot me if I'm late for services."

"Tomorrow, then? After school?"

I pull my hand away. "I'll think about it." I slide into the chapel before he can protest.

I spend the entire meeting watching Jarod out of the corner of my eye, wondering what he wanted to say. I know better than to jump every time he beckons, but tomorrow can't come soon enough.

I shove a bite of my brownie sundae into my mouth and smile at Amy when she comes by to check on us. She smiles back at me and shakes her head at Jarod. Even she can tell I'm crushing on the wrong boy, and this "date" is not going well at all.

When he said we needed to talk, I convinced myself that he was finally giving up on Laina. I thought he wanted to talk about the kiss and everything that went wrong afterward. But we've been sitting here for nearly half an hour, and he hasn't shut up about Laina yet. And that's on top of the time he spent talking about her while we drove all the way out here.

"Did you hear that Rachel Nichols broke up with Crawford?" Jarod asks. "Now, there's nothing to stop him from going after Laina. Not that a girlfriend would have stopped a creep like him, but at least Laina wouldn't fall for his act when he was still dating someone else."

I smile and nod and take another bite of ice cream. I want to reach across the table and shake him and tell him to wake up, because Laina might not be the perfect angel he thinks she is, and she's so in love with Shane that she'll probably never notice Jarod, no matter what he does. But one mistake is hardly a reason for crucifying her. And if he knew that Shane kissed Laina before breaking up with Rachel, Jarod would just get all over-protective and more determined than ever to prove that he's the one she needs.

"So we're going to sit here complaining about life being unfair?" I ask.

"No." Jarod grins and reaches across the table to squeeze my hand. "We're going to step up our game. We have to show Crawford that he's not going to win."

I pull my hand away and run my fingers through my hair, trying to ignore the tingles running up my arm. "First of all, no girl really wants to have guys fighting over her like she's some kind of prize. Laina's a person, not a trophy. And you're going to lose her entirely if you don't stop treating her like the toy at the bottom of your cereal box. She doesn't belong to you."

Jarod's eyes narrow. "Are you saying that Crawford won before I got a chance to play the game?"

I push my ice cream dish aside and stand up. "I'm saying Laina's a person, not a pet. And if you don't drop this macho-jerk-from-the-nineteen-fifties act, you'll never have a chance!"

I realize that I'm screaming, and the three other customers in the diner are staring at me. I don't care. I grab my purse and my jacket, and I storm outside.

As soon as I reach the nearly empty parking lot, I realize how stupid my little temper tantrum was. I don't have a car, and it's more than thirty miles back to the edge of town. And I can't call anyone for a ride, because my parents totally live in the dark ages, and they refuse to get me my own cell phone. All I have is a pay-as-you-go phone, and it's out of minutes.

Amy would probably let me use the phone behind the counter, but walking back inside now would completely ruin my grand exit. Besides, I can already feel the tears streaming down my cheeks and I don't really want to face Jarod looking like this.

I take a deep breath and hold my head up high as I stride across the parking lot. Maybe a thirty-mile walk will be good for me. I should probably exercise more anyway.

Or maybe I'll get lucky and someone will give me a ride home.

"Where are you going?" Jarod's fingers close around my arm, and he pulls me back to the row of dilapidated benches outside the door of the diner. He tries to get me to sit down, but I refuse. "You don't think you're going to walk home, do you?"

I pull away and cross my arms. "In case you haven't noticed, I don't belong to you, either."

The tears are gushing by now, and Jarod reaches out to wipe them away. I slap his hand and grab a tissue out of my purse to wipe my own eyes.

"I'm sorry," he says. "I don't know what I did, but whatever it was, I'm sorry."

I sniffle and shake my head. Of course he doesn't know why I'm crying. I'm not even sure myself. I don't know what hurts worse: the fact that Jarod can't see why turning my sister into the prize in a stupid pissing contest with Shane Crawford is a bad thing, or the fact that he's never even thought about fighting for me.

"Come on," Jarod says. "Let's finish our sundaes before they melt, and you can tell me how to get Laina's attention without making a complete fool of myself."

I take a deep breath and shake my head. I don't trust myself to speak without losing it again. But I can't play matchmaker anymore.

A semi-familiar car pulls into the parking lot, and Dave climbs out of it. "Sorry, Jar," I say. "I can't do this right now. My ride is here." I jog across the parking lot and reach Dave as he's locking the doors. I turn my back to Jarod, so he won't see the pleading look on my face while I beg Dave to play along.

"Are you here by yourself?" I ask. "I mean, I can see that you're alone right at this moment, but are you meeting someone, or could you do a huge favor for me?"

"Well, I was supposed to meet my sister, but I'm early." He glances over my shoulder to where Jarod is still standing next to the door of the diner. "Let me guess. You had a fight with your boyfriend, and now you need a ride home?"

"Yes. Well, no. Kind of, I guess. Yes, we got in a fight. No, he's not my boyfriend. We're friends. Sort of. But I really don't want to talk to him right now, and I kind of already told him that you were here to give me a ride home, and if I don't get into the car with you in the next thirty seconds, he's going to know I lied, and can you give me a ride home or not?"

Dave smiles and shakes his head before unlocking his car and opening the passenger-side door for me. "I guess Amy won't mind if I make her wait a little bit. I wouldn't want to make you look like a liar in front of your ... are you sure he's not your boyfriend?"

I climb in, and I wait until he slides behind the wheel and starts the car before I respond. "Of course I'm sure. How could someone not know if she had a boyfriend?" I resist the urge to look in the rearview mirror as Dave pulls out of the parking lot. Jarod is probably already back inside, polishing off both ice cream sundaes, but in case he's still watching, I don't really want to see the look on his face.

Dave laughs. "No, that's not what I meant. I saw you guys here a couple of weeks ago, and you looked … the way he looked at you, the way you looked at each other, I thought …" He shakes his head. "Does Mr. Just-a-Friend know he's not your boyfriend?"

"Trust me, he knows," I say. "Jarod does not want to be my boyfriend."

"But you want to be his girlfriend, right?"

"What? No! Of course not. We're friends."

"You really believe that, huh?" He grins. "I'm sorry to tell you, but that's impossible."

I fold my arms across my chest and lean back in my seat, refusing to dignify that remark with an answer. But after driving for thirty minutes in total silence, I have to ask. "Why is it so impossible to believe that someone would want to be friends with me?"

"Because." Dave glances at me quickly before turning his attention back to the road. "You're too beautiful to be someone that any guy is 'just friends' with. And in my experience, a girl doesn't get so upset by something that one of her 'friends' says that she has to go driving away with the first hot guy she sees, to make her 'friend' jealous." He laughs. "Don't get me wrong. I'm flattered that you chose me to make him jealous, but you are not just friends."

"You are so far off base it's not even funny," I say. "I didn't choose you. You were the only one around, and I needed to get out of there. And Jarod is in love with Laina. He doesn't even think about me that way."

"He doesn't think of you in what way?"

"You know, like a girl. I'm just a little sister."

"But you're not his sister," Dave says as he pulls into my driveway. "So unless he's gay, and I'm guessing he's not if you say he's in love with Alaina, he thinks of you that way. He's a guy. It's built into our genetic code. It's not a choice. It's a reflex."

"Whatever. Jarod so doesn't want a relationship with me."

"So he's only attracted to you if he wants a relationship? What if he just thinks you're hot?"

"Then I guess it's a good thing that I don't think of him that way, isn't it?"

"If you say so."

I roll my eyes and climb out of the car. "Thanks for the ride. I guess I'll see you in school tomorrow?"

"Yep. First period. It's a date." He winks. "Bye, sexy."

I laugh and blow him a kiss as he pulls out of the driveway.

Chapter Fourteen

Jarod's car whips into the driveway, tires squealing, and he jumps out almost before the car stops moving. "Don't you ever do something like that again! Did you even know that guy?"

I lean against the railing on the porch steps and pick at my peeling fingernail polish, trying to look bored. "Of course I know him. That was Dave. We've only been going to school together since second grade. I'm not stupid enough to get into a car with someone I don't know." He doesn't need to know I was seriously considering hitchhiking before Dave showed up.

I yawn and glance at my watch.

"Well, next time you get mad at me for no reason, could you please talk to me about it, instead of driving off with some guy I've never met who could be a serial killer for all I know and scaring me half to death?"

"Cut the drama, Jar. First of all, you know Dave. He's

been going to school with us forever, he helped out with Laina's clothing drive, and he's Amy's little brother. It's not like I took off with some psychopath." I take a deep breath and exhale slowly. "And secondly, you don't really care. You're only annoyed because you didn't get to have the last word. But that is so not my problem. Find someone else to help you measure your manhood against Shane. I am beyond through with you."

I spin on my heel and storm up the steps to the front door. But I drop my key as I'm fumbling to unlock the door, and it slips through a crack in the porch. I drop to my knees, blinking back tears. I can see the key, glinting in the fading sunlight, completely out of reach and mocking me. Once again, my perfect exit is ruined, and I'm stuck.

"I care." Jarod kneels beside me and lifts my chin so that my eyes meet his. "I do care about you. You're my best friend." He takes my hand and leads me to the swing on the opposite side of the porch. He wraps his arms around me and runs his fingers through my hair. I lean my head against his shoulder and remind myself not to cry, even though all I want to do is sob uncontrollably.

His arms tighten around me, and he rubs my back, slowly rocking the swing back and forth. "You want to tell me what's really wrong?" he asks. "What was that blow-up at the diner all about?"

I shake my head, too embarrassed to say anything. I knew from the start that I didn't stand a chance. Jarod has always had his heart set on Laina, and I'll never be able to compete with her.

Jarod kisses the top of my head and sighs. "I hate seeing you like this," he says. "Please talk to me. Let me fix it."

"I can't." My tears spill over, running down my cheeks and soaking the shoulder of Jarod's coat. "You can't." I rub my eyes and sit up, pulling myself out of his embrace. "We can't fix this. I need you to leave. Please."

He brushes away the tears running down my cheek and caresses my cheek. "I'm not leaving until you tell me what's bothering you. Please let me help." He leans in until his lips brush softly against mine, and I want to melt into him and forget about this whole, crappy day. I wrap my arms around his neck and twine my fingers in his hair to pull him closer. But as his lips crush against mine, I stiffen and pull away.

"What are you doing?" I ask.

Jarod smiles. "I'm trying to kiss you." He inches closer, but I put both hands on his muscular chest and push him away.

"Why?"

He sits back and looks at me, arching one eyebrow. "What?"

"Why do you want to kiss me? Why now?"

"Why not?"

"Seriously?" I laugh bitterly and slide to the opposite side of the swing, turning my body to face him and pulling my knees up onto the seat to create a physical barrier between us. "You spent the entire afternoon whining about how much you want Laina. You really think kissing me is the answer?"

He runs his fingers through his hair in that adorable way he always does when he's nervous. "I don't know. I guess not."

"You don't know? Really? Come on, Jar. I may not get perfect grades, but even I'm smart enough to know that's a load of crap. You can't actually believe that Laina would be okay with it if she came home right now to find us making out on the front porch."

He shrugs.

"Oh. My. Goldfish. You want her to see us kissing, don't you? You're hoping she'll come home and catch us, so she'll be jealous and choose you instead of Shane. You're using me to get to her." My stomach churns and I swallow hard to keep myself from throwing up.

"What? No!" Jarod's face pales and he shakes his head violently. "No, of course not. We can't get caught. She wouldn't understand."

I fold my arms and glare. "I don't understand either."

This is where a dramatic exit might be really effective, but of course I have nowhere to go. Besides, I really want to hear his answer.

"I know," he says. "You're amazing, Andi. And beautiful. And one of the best people I know. I don't want to hurt you. You know that, right?"

"Yet, you'll kiss me and make me think you're totally into me, when the whole time, you're pretending that I'm Laina. In case you didn't know, that kind of hurts, Jar."

"I wasn't pretending anything. I'm not sorry I kissed you. You looked so beautiful, and your lips were so soft, and … and I admit, the timing was wrong. But I wasn't thinking about Laina. It was all you."

"You called me Laina, Bozo. I think it's pretty obvious that you were thinking about her."

He gulps. "Yeah, that was an accident. Can't we forget about that?"

"It's not exactly something you forget."

"I know." He runs his fingers through his hair and exhales forcefully. "I'm stupid. It's just, I've been in love with Laina forever. But you …" He reaches across the seat and takes my hand. "I don't know. Sometimes, it feels like you know me better than anyone else."

I pull my hand away.

Jarod stands up and paces back and forth across the porch, finally stopping beside the swing. He leans against the porch rail and studies my face. "I don't know. Laina and me, we … I mean, she … Well, you know. I love her. I always have." He sighs. "But I like you, too. A lot. I don't want to mess up our friendship." He sits beside me again. "It's just, sometimes, when I'm with you, I get so confused."

"Well, until you figure things out, could you please keep your lips to yourself?"

Jarod blushes. "It's a deal." He stares at me for a minute longer, then shakes his head and smiles. "So do you want to keep sitting out here on the porch until someone else gets home, or can I be your knight in shining armor by crawling under the porch to find your key?"

Ten minutes later, I hang my coat on the hook inside the front door and say goodbye to Jarod.

"I know I'm not going to get a goodnight kiss, but can I at least hug you?" he asks.

I point to the cobwebs covering his jacket and in his hair. "Not a chance. I'm not a big fan of spiders."

I watch him walk back to his car and drive away, and then I go to my room, where I climb into bed and pull the covers up over my head. Maybe tomorrow will be less complicated.

"Don't look now," Emily whispers, "but Dave is totally staring at you. Poor boy is practically drooling."

I glance across the room, because that's the first thing you always do when someone tells you not to look. Dave doesn't blush or look away like a normal person would. Instead, he blows a kiss.

"Oh my Godiva, Andi, you're blushing," Emily says. "I never thought I'd see the day when some boy could make you lose your cool." She giggles loudly, ending with a high-pitched squeal.

Mr. Mayer looks up from the stack of papers he's grading and clears his throat. "If you have a question about Pearl Harbor, Miss Nichols, I'd be happy to answer it for you.

But please allow Miss Andersen to concentrate on her own work."

Emily blushes. "Sorry, Mr. Mayer," she mumbles.

She waits until he's turned his attention back to his grade book before she whispers again. "Is there something going on with you two?"

"Me and Mr. Mayer? No way." I ignore her exasperated scowl and turn my full attention to my textbook, and the worksheet Mr. Mayer wants us to complete. Worksheets like this usually take me all of two seconds to finish, but I can't concentrate on the sinking of the Arizona. I'm suddenly aware of Dave's far-too-intense gaze, and it takes everything I have not to stare right back at him.

I know I'm not fooling Emily for a second, but she doesn't dare say anything else now that Mr. Mayer is paying attention. She'll pounce as soon as class is over. Which means I have only ten minutes to figure out which version of the story to tell. Because of course I'm going to tell her about my crappy day yesterday. Only, it will have to be a slightly modified version, because no one, not even Emily, needs to hear about what happened between me and Jarod.

I can't help hearing FDR's voice echoing in my head. Last night was truly "a date which will live in infamy."

I glance across the room at Dave and wonder what I'll have to do to make sure he tells the same version of the story.

Chapter Fifteen

As soon as the bell rings, Emily grabs my arm and pulls me to the south stairs, which only lead to the home economics and shop classrooms. It's our favorite spot for private conversations because the stairs are almost always empty. Summer joins us as we pass her first period class.

"Okay, spill," Emily says, as soon as we're alone in the stairwell. "I want the whole story, but make it quick. I can't be late to math again, or Mr. Rosenquist says he'll call my parents."

I laugh. "Then go to class. We can talk at lunch. I promise."

"No way," Summer insists. "You have to fill us in. Yesterday, you barely even knew Dave was alive, and now you're blushing when you catch him looking at you? What happened last night?"

I bite my lip. I totally need more time to come up with a good version of the story. "Really, guys, it's not as huge as you think it is. Dave gave me a ride home, and we talked. We may have flirted a little, tiny bit. He's nice. But he's with Heather and you know I would never trespass on someone else's territory." Well, at least, not usually.

"Oh. My. Gorilla. You didn't hear?" Emily's voice lowers to a whisper as she slips into "juicy gossip" mode, and I have to lean in to hear what she's saying. "Heather dumped Dave. Hard. He was supposed to pick her up from work on Saturday night, but he was, like, three and a half hours late or something crazy like that." She pauses for effect and then grins wickedly. "I heard he was off driving around town with some other girl all night long."

I inhale sharply and choke on my own breath. "Really?" I finally manage to squeak out. "That's insane."

Emily grins and leans forward, obviously pleased with my reaction. "Seriously. Who would've thought Dorky Dave could be such a ladies' man?"

I cough and grab a mint out of my purse, taking my time to unwrap it before I answer. "I don't know. He's not as dorky as he used to be. I think he's kind of nice." I pop the mint into my mouth and bite into it, grateful that Emily didn't guess the real reason for my little choking fit.

"He sounds like a jerk," Summer says. "Andi, I'd be careful. You really don't want to get with a guy that cheats. Trust me. You don't want to get involved with someone, hoping to reform them. People don't change. The only one you have control over is yourself."

I roll my eyes. Sometimes, I think Summer takes her support group stuff way too seriously. "I already told you it was nothing. He gave me a ride home. That's it. It's not like I'm planning to run off and have his babies or something." I force my voice to remain neutral. "And maybe he had a perfectly good reason for being one hour late to pick Heather up on Saturday. Maybe we forgot to look at the clock and totally lost track of time." I can feel my cheeks getting hot as soon as I realize my slip-up, but luckily, the warning bell rings and Emily doesn't even catch my mistake.

"Crap, I'm late!" She sprints off down the hall, plowing through the still-crowded hallway.

Summer giggles and grabs my arm. "So you're the mystery girl Dave blew off Heather for last weekend, huh?"

I shake my head, and she laughs. "Don't worry, your secret's safe with me. Come on. You can tell me the rest of the story in Spanish class. I heard Señor Astrakhan isn't here today, and the sub is playing a movie."

We claim the last two empty desks in the back of the classroom and push them together so that no one will overhear our whispered conversation. And I tell Summer the whole story. Minus the Jarod parts.

"So I don't know. I think Dave was definitely flirting with me, but he didn't even tell me that he wasn't with Heather anymore, so he couldn't have been too serious, right?" I shake my head. "Not that I care. I'm so not looking for a boyfriend right now. I'm really tired of being the second choice, you know?"

Summer snorts and then quickly covers her mouth and ducks her head when the sour old substitute glares at us. "When have you ever been second place? The rest of us have to scavenge from your leftovers."

"I don't think you get to complain about my leftovers when you've been dating Josh since the Snow Ball, and I never even went out with him."

"You know what I mean." She glares at me in an if-I-didn't-love-you-I'd-totally-want-to-barf kind of way. "How many guys have you turned down for the prom so far this year?"

"Three. But Rob only asked me because he was trying to make Laina jealous. He kept staring at her the entire time we were talking."

"That's just because Laina's got big boobs. I keep

telling you, not all guys are that shallow. Some of them really do notice other things." She shrugs. "I'd kill to have your hair. And you have that adorable nose, unlike my huge honker, and you're so stinking skinny, even though you never stop eating."

"Yeah, well Laina also has gorgeous hair, and she's got an amazing body under those baggy clothes she wears, and every boy in school is freaking in love with her."

"You're imagining things, and I still think you're nuts for turning Rob down, but whatever. You've turned down three offers. How many guys have even asked your sister to the prom? None? That's what I thought."

"It's not like we're keeping score," I say. "Besides, who says no one has asked Laina to the prom? She might have turned down fifteen different boys for all we know."

Summer sighs. "Okay, then who went to the prom with the captain of the varsity football team when she was only a freshman? You or your sister? And who had to choose between five totally hot guys last year? And which one of you had to get special permission to go to the Northridge prom when she was only in eighth grade, because her boyfriend was a senior? Oh yeah. All you."

"Yeah, but that's not the point."

"If it's not a competition, then why are you so worried about being in second place? You have plenty of guys to choose from. Stop comparing yourself to your sister."

My shoulders slump. "When it really matters, Laina's the one he goes for every single time." I think of Jarod's confession last night, and I almost wish I'd let him kiss me. I may never get another chance.

"Wow," Summer says. "You really have it bad for this guy, don't you? I've never seen you so worked up about a boy. Like, ever."

"What? Who?" I blink rapidly. "Oh. Dave. Right. Yeah, well, he makes me laugh. And he's kind of cute, don't you think? So, yeah. Dave." I hesitate. I don't want to declare my undying love and devotion to Dave. Maybe he's not as creepy as I thought, but he's nothing like Jarod.

Although maybe that's a good thing.

Summer grins. "I totally knew it. You're hooked. I've never seen you this distracted by a guy. But don't worry. If Emily's right about the way he was looking at you during first period, you have nothing to fear. He's totally hooked on you, too." She shimmies in her seat. "I sit right next to him in English. I'll talk to him for you, okay?"

I think about protesting, but really, it's easier to let her think I was talking about Dave than trying to explain my mystery crush. So I don't say anything.

The bell rings, and Summer sprints for the door. If I know her, I'll be practically engaged by lunchtime.

It could be worse. Dave may not be super-hot, like Jarod or even Nick Carver, but he's cute enough, and he did make me laugh. Maybe he'll help me forget Jarod.

I'm completely failing in my attempts to forget him on my own.

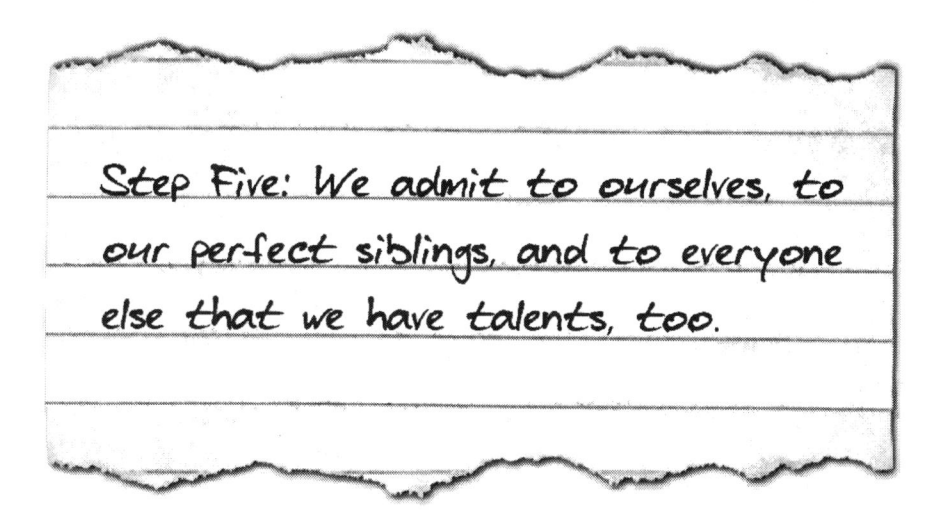

Step Five: We admit to ourselves, to our perfect siblings, and to everyone else that we have talents, too.

Chapter Sixteen

"You're gonna love this," Dave says as we follow the usher to our seats in the Little Community Theater Auditorium.

"I don't know," I say. "I've never been a big fan of musicals. I prefer serious theater, like Shakespeare. I don't get the whole spontaneous, choreographed dance-number thing."

"But that's part of the magic."

"Really? What's magical about singing and dancing and jumping over tables in the cafeteria? Am I supposed to be impressed that no one gets in trouble? Where is the principal? And where are the bad dancers? Do you really believe that every single person in that high school was a classically trained dancer? There isn't a single kid with two left feet?"

Dave laughs. "Maybe the bad dancers run and hide when the music starts."

"Okay, so how does everyone know all of the words to the song, as soon as the main character makes them up? Are they psychics as well as professional singers and dancers?

Where do they hide the full orchestra that kicks in whenever they feel musically inclined? And if they're so freaking talented, what are they doing wasting their time in some Podunk high school in the middle of nowhere? Why haven't they banded together to take over Broadway? Musicals are so unrealistic."

"Really? You never break into spontaneous song with all of your friends as backup dancers when you eat a particularly delicious tuna salad sandwich? Happens to me all the time."

The lights dim and the audience grows quiet before I can think of a witty response, so I settle back into my seat and turn my attention to the stage. Dave leans across the armrest and whispers, "I think you'll like this one, though. *The Phantom of the Opera* is in a class of its own."

Music fills the theater as the orchestra plays the opening notes, and the curtain rises to reveal a dusty, old-timey theater. In the dim light, a group of performers appears in the middle of the stage. I can't really figure out what's going on, though. It almost seems like they've started in the middle of the play or something. I lean over to ask Dave if we missed the first act. But then, some guy calls for "a little illumination," and a chandelier in the middle of the stage blazes to life.

The orchestra strikes up a haunting melody that chills me straight through, and I lean forward in my seat, totally caught up in the transformation happening onstage. The pale, washed-out lighting gives way to bright spotlights, and I completely forget about Dave and everyone else as I get lost in early twentieth-century Paris. This is so much better than going to the movies. Even Shakespeare might have trouble competing with the haunting melodies.

I didn't think I'd ever miss the theater, but I feel like I could step right into the action, to be a part of Christine's tragic tale.

I haven't set foot in the Little Community Theater since the disastrous last night of *Much Ado About Nothing*, when I tried to tell Jarod that I liked him, but he took off with Laina before I could say anything. In fact, I've avoided all of Jarod's performances since then. I only agreed to this date because Jarod was so busy directing the school play that he didn't try out for *The Phantom of the Opera*.

Three hours later, as the music fades and the curtain drops, Dave squeezes my hand. I look down at our intertwined fingers and wonder how long we've been holding hands.

"This was fun. Thanks." I casually pull my hand away and reach for my purse.

We follow the crowd out of the theater, but Dave stops when we reach the lobby. He pulls me to the side of the room and points to a large poster. "They're holding auditions for *Cinderella* tomorrow morning. You should do it."

"What?" My voice is too loud, and several heads turn in our direction. I wait until they lose interest, and then I try again. "No. Acting's not really my thing, and I don't sing."

He cocks his head to one side and studies me. "Are you trying to be humble, or have you forgotten your spectacular performance as Mavis the singing bullfrog in our fifth grade play?"

I laugh. "That was a long time ago. I don't lounge on lily pads these days. And it's been a long time since anyone other than my showerhead has heard me sing. Even Mavis the bullfrog was totally upstaged by Cyril the dancing chipmunk."

"Well, you have to admit, I was a cute, little rodent," Dave says. "But I only danced. You have a great voice. Come on. You know you want to."

I can feel my cheeks burning under his gaze, and I'm in danger of totally losing my cool. I lean against the wall in my best I'm-so-bored pose, and stifle a pretend yawn. "Really. It's not my thing. This was kind of fun tonight, but I'm not about to go prancing around a stage in a frilly costume, pretending to be someone I'm not. I've outgrown the need for playing make-believe."

"See?" Dave laughs. "You're a natural. You can flip through a repertoire of fake emotions like it's nothing, fooling almost everyone around you into believing that you really mean it. That's acting. Professional quality."

I stand up straight and run my fingers through my hair. "I don't know what you're talking about."

I imagine myself standing center stage, in the middle of a brilliant spotlight, while my friends and family cheer me on from the audience and total strangers adore me from afar. And for a minute, I wonder what it might be like to be the star of the show for once. But I'm not a theater geek. I left that world behind years ago.

Dave laughs. "Which part are you thinking? Cinderella or the evil stepmother?"

I roll my eyes and walk away. "I'm not auditioning."

"Right." He scurries to catch up and slings his arm around my shoulders. "So do you want me to pick you up at ten o'clock tomorrow morning? Auditions start at ten-thirty, and you don't want to be late."

I sigh. "Make it eight. You can at least take me out to breakfast, so it won't be a completely wasted day."

"It's a deal." Dave grins and whistles the theme from *Phantom of the Opera* as we walk across the parking lot to his car.

As soon as he drops me off at home, I grab Mom's laptop and search for videos of *Cinderella*. It turns out, the musical is kind of different from the Disney cartoon. There isn't a single talking mouse or bird with mad sewing skills. I study the different versions of the play, from Julie Andrews to Leslie Ann Warren to Brandy, and even several shaky, out-of-focus videos of community theater productions.

It couldn't hurt to be prepared.

By the time Dave picks me up on Saturday morning, I'm totally ready, and I read through my scene without a single mistake. I can tell the director is impressed, because she has me read through the scene three more times with different guys trying out for Prince Charming. I breeze through the readings with the first two, but I nearly pass out when Jarod walks onstage.

I think I manage to save my butt, though. I turn my initial shock into Cinderella's swoony, melodramatic reaction to meeting Prince Charming, and I manage the rest of the scene without a problem.

I spend the rest of the weekend dreaming of ball gowns and imagining a blossoming romance, both onstage and off, between a certain Prince Charming and a previously-invisible Cinderella. If Jarod has to fall in love with me night after night onstage, he's bound to start seeing me as something more than Laina's little sister in real life.

Dave is a freaking genius!

I pound on the bathroom door, but after a full five minutes with no response from Laina, I pick the lock. They're announcing the *Cinderella* cast list today after school, and I need to look good. I still have to straighten my hair, and Laina's developed a habit of leaving without me if I'm not ready for school on time.

She's sitting on the edge of the tub, wrapped in a towel and staring blankly at the trash can. She doesn't even look up when I push my way into the steam-filled bathroom. Her hair hangs limp and soggy down her back, and she shivers when I turn on the fan. I reach around her and turn off the shower.

"Are you okay?"

She blinks and looks at me, as if she can't figure out where I came from. "I thought the door was locked." She wrings the water out of her hair, leaving a puddle on the floor, and grabs a hairbrush. Flashing a plastic smile at me, she busies herself with applying her makeup and styling her hair.

She avoids making eye contact with her reflection.

"What happened?" I ask.

Laina grabs the hair dryer and turns it on. She shrugs and waves the hair dryer at me. "I can't hear you."

I plug in my straightening iron and lean in to share the mirror. "Are you okay? You look kind of out of it."

"I'm fine. But I have to get ready for school." She drops the hair dryer and runs her fingers through her half-dried hair before sprinting out of the bathroom.

By the time I finish straightening my frizz and throw on some clothes, Laina has already left for school, and I have to beg a ride from Mom. The warning bell rings as we pull into the parking lot, which means I won't have time to search for Laina before first period.

She probably planned it that way.

Chapter Seventeen

Dave waits in the doorway of Mr. Mayer's class. He hands me a single pink rose, and then he grins like a total lunatic when I smile.

"What's this for?" I ask, twirling the rose between my fingers and holding back a sneeze.

"I wanted to see you smile."

"Hmmm ... I guess it worked, then." I take a deep breath and grin.

"So roses aren't your favorite?" Dave asks. "What flower do you prefer?"

My mouth drops open and I blink rapidly. "What?" How in the world did he know I was faking it?

"Don't worry," he says. "Your performance was nearly flawless. You could probably fool just about anyone. I almost even believed you. But you bite your bottom lip and crinkle your nose in the most adorable way when you're faking a smile." He motions to the rose. "It's not what you would pick for yourself, is it?"

I laugh. "Well, actually, no. Pink roses are Laina's signature flower, but I've always thought roses are the snobs of the flower world. I prefer something less pretentious." I bite my lip and try to shove the image of my shattered sister out of my mind. She doesn't want to talk about whatever it is that's bugging her, so what am I supposed to do? It's not like I can force her to confide in me.

"I'll try to remember that," Dave says. He takes my hand and squeezes it softly as we walk into the classroom. "So, are you ready?"

I pull my hand away and wipe it on my jeans, hoping he didn't notice that my palms are sweating. "Ready for what?" I blink innocently and flash my best I'm-totally-clueless smile.

He laughs. "You're good, Andi. I'm telling ya, you're a natural. If I didn't know you so well, I might even believe that you aren't counting the hours until the *Cinderella* cast list is posted. But don't worry. You rocked that audition. You'll definitely get the part."

He smiles and pats my shoulder awkwardly. "So, should we go out for ice cream after school to kill the time while we wait? You know, to keep our minds off the results, so we don't psych ourselves out or anything? Amy says her supreme brownie sundae is the perfect thing for calming nerves."

"Whatever. You didn't even try out for anything, you big chicken. You don't have anything to be nervous about." I flip my hair. "Not that I'm nervous or anything. I only auditioned in the first place so you would stop bugging me. I don't care which part I get." I shove the mental image of me in Cinderella's ball gown aside and push past Dave to get to my seat. "If you're looking for an excuse to ask me out again, just do it."

Dave grins and leans on my desk. "Okay, Andi. Want

to go to the diner with me after school?"

"See? Was that so hard?" I laugh. "I wouldn't mind driving out to say hi to Amy. But no ice cream. I'm thinking chili-cheese fries."

"It's a date. Meet me in front of the school after last period." Dave winks and then saunters across the room to his seat as Mr. Mayer clears his throat and stands up to begin bombarding us with facts about the aftermath of World War Two.

I yawn and lean back in my chair, settling into my I'm-too-cool-for-class persona, but I nearly lose the façade when I notice Dave watching me with a smirk. How does he always know when I'm faking it?

Emily tosses a folded piece of paper onto my desk. I open it carefully, trying not to let the sound of crinkling paper catch Mr. Mayer's attention, and then I spread it out on my notebook so I can read it secretly.

"What's up with you and Dave? Is he officially your boyfriend yet?"

I shake my head in a don't-be-ridiculous kind of way, and Emily hunches over her desk to scribble furiously on another blank sheet of paper. As soon as Mr. Mayer looks down to check his notes, she throws the new page at me.

"What are you waiting for?? You are so into him, don't even try to deny it. Andi Andersen doesn't hang out with the same boy every day for a week if he's not boyfriend material. So go for it already! But don't forget about the rest of us when you slip off into lovey-dovey land, k?"

I turn the paper over and scrawl a quick reply on the back. "You're crazy."

Just because Dave is obviously attracted to me doesn't mean the feelings are mutual. He's been obsessing about me for years, and it hasn't changed my feelings. One date won't magically transform him into the man of my dreams.

I've barely even noticed the sparkle in his chocolate

brown eyes or his adorable dimple. Dave's not boyfriend material. We haven't even kissed.

He hasn't even tried.

I take a deep breath and exhale slowly as Dave pulls into the Little Community Theater parking lot. It doesn't matter which part I get.

"Your audition was flawless," Dave says. "They'd be crazy not to pick you."

"I'm not worried. Do I look worried?" I laugh and slouch against the seat.

"No, you don't look worried at all." Dave grabs my hand and studies my ragged fingernails, running his thumb over the chipped polish. "It's a good thing, too. Some girls bite their nails when they're nervous. You wouldn't want to damage this manicure or anything."

I blush and pull my hand away, tucking my fingers into a fist to conceal my battered nails.

"But if you're really not worried about what part you get, we don't have to stay. My mom's friends with the director. I could call her tomorrow for you."

I pop the latch on my seatbelt and jump out of the car before he can drive away. "No." I sigh. "I might as well get this over with, so you'll stop bugging me."

Dave laughs and follows me into the theater lobby.

"You check in over there," he says, pointing to the crowd of people gathering in front of a long table piled high with stacks of paper. I join the A through L line, while Dave strolls over to a smaller table in the corner to get his assignment for the stage crew.

"Congratulations," says the woman in a too-tight bun and a totally blah, beige suit, after checking my name against the list on her clipboard. She pulls a script out of a large box sitting on the table beside her and hands it to me. "Your lines are already highlighted." She grabs a packet of papers with my name in big, bold letters on the top of the first sheet. "Here is the rehearsal schedule, and all the information you'll need for costume fittings and performances. Be sure to fill out the form on the last page of your information packet if you'd like your two complimentary tickets for the friends and family special matinee performance."

She tucks the stack of papers into my script and hands the whole thing to me. "Please read through your part to familiarize yourself with the lines prior to our first cast meeting on Saturday at three o'clock. Be prepared to ask any questions you may have at that time." She waves me away and turns her attention to the next person in line.

I step back from the table as the middle-aged man behind me gives his name and fidgets nervously while beige bun lady checks her clipboard. "I'm so sorry," she says. "You're not on my list, Mr. Christofferson. However, we still need a few extra hands on our stage crew, if you're interested."

The poor man looks crushed as he shuffles away from the table empty-handed. I clutch my script and exhale slowly. I'd never considered the very real chance that I might not get a part.

"So? What part did you get?" Dave asks, reaching for my script.

"Oh, she didn't say." I resist the urge to yank the script out of his hands. "But she said my lines were already highlighted in there, so I guess it should be easy to figure out."

I watch Dave flipping through my script and carefully keep my expression blank as I study his reactions. I tell myself not to get my hopes up, but the smile on his face tells me all of my worries and doubts were totally unnecessary. I totally nailed the audition.

"Wow. Congrats," Dave says and offers the script to me. "You'll be amazing."

I take it and eagerly scan the opening pages for my first line. The highlighted lines are easy to find. I flip through the whole script, and then pull out the packet of loose papers that are tucked into the back.

I can't play this part.

"Hey, Andi." Jarod's voice pulls me away from my panicked thoughts. "Are you my Cinderella?"

I blush and drop my gaze. Of course Jarod would be Prince Charming. I study the fancy tile patterns on the floor of the lobby, searching for the right words.

"Is that a yes? Are you my happily ever after?"

Glancing up at Jarod's smiling face, I shake my head slightly. He's only teasing, but there's a hint of real question in his eyes. We haven't really talked in more than a week. Not since I told him to leave me alone until he figured things out. The way he's looking at me now, I wonder if he's decided.

My heart flutters with the barest glimmer of hope. Maybe I could be his real-life fairy tale. "Should I try on the slipper to see if it fits?"

"Actually," Dave says, slipping his arm around my waist and taking a step forward, to stand between Jarod and me, "I think I heard that girl in the Northridge cheerleader uniform say she's Cinderella." He points across the room to a girl who could almost give Laina a run for her money in the looks department. She's not quite Barbie doll perfect, but definitely cheerleader cliché.

Jarod frowns. "What part did you get?"

"Andi's going to be playing stepsister number one. The hot one." Dave smiles and squeezes my hand.

I toss my hair over my shoulder nonchalantly. "Well, I

could definitely make the wicked stepsister totally sexy, but I don't know if I'm even going to take the part. I only tried out because Dave kind of pushed me into it. But I'm really busy. I don't think I'll have time for all of the practices." I wave the rehearsal schedule in front of me and let out an I-really-wish-my-life-wasn't-so-busy sigh. "I might pass on the whole thing."

I play the unwanted sister every day of my life. I don't want to be that girl on stage as well.

"You have to do this with me," Jarod says. "Remember how much fun we had backstage when we did *Much Ado About Nothing*?"

Dave glares at Jarod and takes both of my hands in his, pulling me around to face him. "You shouldn't do it for him or for me or for anyone else," he says. "Do it because you want to."

"So if I say it's not my thing, you'll stop bugging me about it and leave me alone?"

"If you can honestly say that it's not for you, then I promise not to say another word."

I bite my lip. The stepsister has almost no time on stage with the Prince, and Jarod and I won't even be rehearsing most of our scenes at the same time. But I do miss the stage.

Dave smiles. "You'll be the first stepsister in the history of the story to steal the spotlight away from Cinderella."

I shake my head. "I don't think I can even make it to all of the practices. I live all the way across town, and my sister won't want to chauffer me around every day for weeks."

"No problem," he says. "I already signed up to be on the stage crew, so I have to be here every day anyway. You can ride with me."

"Please?" Jarod says, pulling me away from Dave. "I miss my backstage buddy. It's never the same without you."

I totally forget everyone around us as he takes my hand and stares into my eyes. Maybe playing the forgotten sister won't be so bad. And Dave might be right. This could be the first time in history when Prince Charming chooses the stepsister over the old Cinderella cliché.

Dave clears his throat, and I pull my hand back, breaking the spell Jarod has over me.

"Okay, fine. Since you begged so nicely and all, I guess I'll do it." I glance across the room at the Northridge cheerleader. "But maybe someone should warn poor Cinderella that she doesn't stand a chance. The Prince seems to think her stepsister is totally charming."

Chapter Eighteen

Summer and Emily meet me after last period. We're supposed to start looking for prom dresses, so we can find something good before all of the best dresses are snatched up, but the only dress I can think of is the Cinderella ball gown I won't be wearing. I'm totally lost in my own thoughts and not paying attention to my friends' conversation, until Summer laughs and grabs my arm. "I knew that break-up wouldn't last," she says. "Didn't I tell you they'd get back together?"

"They're not back together. They're just going to prom. As friends." Emily rolls her eyes. "Rachel didn't want her dress to go to waste, and they already had everything planned, so it made sense."

I stop walking and pull my arm away from Summer. "Rachel? Who is she going to prom with?"

Emily sighs. "I don't know why we even try to talk to you anymore. You never listen."

"Sorry." I flash my puppy dog pout and bat my

eyelashes at her. "I promise you have my full attention now. What did I miss?"

"Nothing," Summer says. "I'm just surprised that Rachel and Shane are still going to prom. Honestly, I kind of expected him to ask your sister out. Have you seen the way he stares at her? It's like borderline stalkerish."

I laugh and shake my head, carefully concealing the panic building in my chest. Laina's expecting a prom invitation from Shane, too. She's going to be crushed, and it's all my fault. I'm gonna kill that boy, next time I see him, but in the meantime, I have to fix this before Laina finds out.

We pile into Summer's car, and Emily starts babbling about some stupid thing Nick said last period. When I'm sure enough time has passed that they've forgotten our prom conversation, I gasp and frantically pull a random notebook out of my bag. "Guys! Why didn't you remind me that today is Wednesday?"

I open the notebook and start flipping through pages, pretending to read. "I have that biology test tomorrow, and I don't even know what it's about." I lean forward and grab Summer's shoulder. "You have to drop me at home. Mom will kill me if I fail another test, and I'm supposed to meet Dave later, so I've got to study now."

"Are you sure?" Summer asks. "Dave could probably give you the answers. He aced bio last year. And you need something hot to wear for your date."

I roll my eyes. "It's not a date. Dave's never seen the Julie Andrews version of *Cinderella*, so we're going to watch it and compare interpretations. He's helping me with my part. That's it."

Emily laughs. "No one's ever seen the Julie Andrews version. If you don't want people to know you're hooking up with Dave, fine. But you should come up with a better cover story."

"Whatever, Em." Summer pulls into my driveway, and

I'm halfway out of the car before it stops moving. "I'll call you later."

"You better call," Summer says. "I want to hear every detail of your non-date."

I nod and wave as Summer backs out of the driveway and zooms down the street.

Racing into the house, I drop my coat and backpack on the living room couch, and grab the phone on my way through the kitchen. When I reach Laina's bedroom door, I stop and take a deep breath. I hope Dave's right about my natural acting abilities, because if I don't get this right, Laina might never forgive me.

I bounce into her room without bothering to knock, calling upon every ounce of my bubbly, ditzy persona. "You should get Jarod to take you to the prom. I bet he looks super-hot in a tuxedo." I shove aside a wave of jealousy and plaster a genuine-looking smile across my face. Jarod is the only guy Laina would even consider as a prom alternative, so it has to be him.

I toss the phone at her, and it lands neatly in her lap. She closes the book she's reading and picks at the fuzzy fabric on the arm of her reading chair, shaking her head. "I'm not begging my friend for a pity date."

I force a giggle and flop onto her bed. "Not a pity date. A totally yummy date. You and Jarod would be so cute together." Maybe, if they go to prom, Laina's obsession with Shane will make the night awkward enough that Jarod will finally give up on her. And if they end up together instead, at least I'll know he's made a choice.

Laina puts her book down and crosses the room to sit on the bed beside me, dropping the phone onto the middle of her fluffy comforter. "What's the deal? Last week, you were all convinced that Shane and I should get together."

I roll over onto my stomach and kick my legs up in the air. "You deserve the whole cliché prom experience. Limo, fancy dinner, totally hot date in a tuxedo. And you know you'll hang out with Jarod all night anyway. Might as well make it official."

"I'll have all of that stuff when I go to the prom with Shane."

I should have known better than to trust Emily's expired information.

"Oh. My. Gobstopper. When did he ask, and why didn't you tell me?" I grab Mr. Cuddles from her pillow and hug him tightly. This means I don't have to force Jarod and Laina together after all. And maybe it's not too late for a miracle of my own.

Laina squirms. "Well, he hasn't technically asked yet, but he will. He was sick and he missed a few days' school, and he's been crazy busy with make-up work since he got back. But he broke up with Rachel, so he obviously doesn't have a date anymore. And you keep saying that Shane's secretly in love with me."

I roll my eyes. "Of course he's in love with you. That doesn't mean he's not stupid. I'm pretty sure he's heard of a little thing called a telephone. He probably even has one of his very own. He could have called you. But he didn't. Because he's a freaking idiot. So quit waiting for Prince Not-So-Charming to get a clue, and go to the prom with Jarod." I take a deep breath, remind myself that this is all for a good cause, and then I pick up the phone, slipping back into my bubbly voice. "I'll call him for you, k?"

She grabs the phone, pushes me off the bed, and glares. "Shane. Broke. Up. With. Rachel. For me." She tosses the phone back onto the bed, folds her arms across her chest, and smiles triumphantly.

I cross my legs and bury my fingers in the carpet, avoiding eye contact. But this is not the time for wallowing in self-pity. Laina was actually smiling and laughing again today. She has to move on before she finds out Shane already has. "If he hasn't asked you by now, he's not going to, no matter how much he likes you. Call Jarod."

Laina's confident smile crumples.

"Never mind," I say. "Ignore me. Shane probably hasn't asked you yet because he's afraid you'll shoot him down or something. Want me to call him?" I pick up the phone and stand up, taking a step back from the bed. Lover boy has some explaining to do.

Laina lunges before I can finish dialing and wrestles the phone away. "I don't need your help." She hugs the phone to her chest and buries her face in her pillow.

"I'm sorry."

When she doesn't respond, I leave the room. That was a total disaster.

Laina grabs me on the way to the cafeteria on Friday and drags me to the empty girls' bathroom next to the south stairs. She sobs for a full five minutes before she pulls herself together enough to tell me that she overheard Shane and Ryan talking about their plans for prom night.

"He's going with Rachel. They're getting back together, and I am so stupid!"

I let my jaw drop and open my eyes wide in apparent shock, tossing in a sharp gasp for good measure. "But they're only going as friends, right?"

"No one goes to prom with someone they only want to be friends with. I may be stupid, but I'm not dumb."

I hug her and hand her a tissue. "Of course they do. Last year, I went with Nick, and we've never been together."

She scoffs. "Yeah, there was never anything going on

with you two at all. That's why you got in-school suspension last semester when Mrs. Gardner caught you making out at the park when you were supposed to be in third period."

"Whatever. Can I help it if he's more fun than Mr. Keeler's boring lectures? Besides, that was months ago. And kissing someone doesn't mean you want to be with them. Sometimes a kiss is totally meaningless."

Laina slumps against the bathroom wall. "Right. One kiss doesn't mean anything. I was so stupid to think Shane liked me."

I shake my head frantically. "That's not what I meant. I wasn't talking about you." Laina shrugs and my protests die on my lips. "He doesn't deserve you anyway."

I'm going to destroy Shane Crawford.

She sniffles and smiles and dries her eyes. "I really wish I could believe that." She takes a deep breath and glances in the mirror to straighten her hair, and then she turns to look at me. "You're not gonna tell anyone I thought he wanted me, right? This is our little secret. Promise?"

I nod. Laina runs her fingers through her long, blonde curls and brushes a speck of imaginary lint from her shirt. Then, she slaps a perfect imitation of a smile on her face and we stroll to the cafeteria together.

Luckily, she's a pretty crier. Miss Perfect's plastic Barbie doll shell doesn't get all red and blotchy and puffy like real people do when they cry. She smiles and nods at Shane and his friends as she saunters past them.

I'm not the only natural actress in the family.

Chapter Nineteen

The lady with the bun who was handing out scripts and schedules on Tuesday afternoon claps her hands and motions for us all to gather around. "Attention please! We have a lot of ground to cover today, and not much time to do it in."

A scrawny guy with oversized glasses and big ears stands beside her, balancing a stack of papers and a large coffee cup in his hands. He reminds me of a Chihuahua, shaking like a leaf as he follows her around the stage. He nods and grunts as she tosses out random comments about the way one girl styles her hair or the way another is standing.

Bun lady stops pacing and takes the coffee cup from Chihuahua boy. "Are you writing this down, Curtis?"

Chihuahua boy whimpers. "I, um, I had my hands full." He stares at his feet, and bun lady sighs.

"Never mind. We'll get to all that later." She frowns and scrutinizes us with cold, grey eyes. I square my shoulders and stare back at her, refusing to let her get to me, but I totally see why Curtis is afraid. This lady is scary.

"I'm Mrs. Mason," bun lady says. She takes a long drink from her coffee cup, watching us over the rim. "*Cinderella* is my seventeenth production for the Little Community Theater, and I've never had a failed show. I don't intend to start now." She glares at us and then points over her shoulder. "This is Curtis Patrick, my intern. He will be assisting me and choreographing the dance numbers."

Curtis waves hesitantly, but he doesn't speak. He looks like he wants the floor to open up and swallow him whole. I wonder why he got into directing in the first place. It doesn't seem like the right job for such a timid guy. If he can't hack it in a small community theater in Podunkville, Wyoming, then he'll never be able to make it in the real world.

I turn my attention back to Mrs. Mason, who is still lecturing us in her sharp, no-nonsense voice. "You have been chosen for your parts because you showed me in the auditions that you have potential, but no matter which role you have been assigned, none of you are stars. I will not have any divas in my show, do you understand?" She pauses and glances around the stage, but no one moves or speaks.

"What I mean, of course," Mrs. Mason says, "is that the actor and actress playing the lead roles are no more important to a great show than the actors and actresses in supporting roles." She pulls a page off the top of Curtis' stack of papers and waves it at us. "I have at least fifty other people here who would love to take your place. Every single one of you can be replaced." She looks around, making eye contact with each of us one-by-one. "If you think you're special, I invite you to leave right now, because this is an ensemble performance. Do you understand?"

Everyone nods, and we shuffle closer together. Jarod takes my hand and squeezes it, and I smile up at him. And I catch Dave watching me from backstage, where he's meeting with the rest of the stage crew. At least I won't have to face

Mrs. Mason alone.

The stage falls silent as Mrs. Mason stares us down, daring us to rise to her challenge.

After a full minute of silence, she grins and reaches up to release her tight bun. Her grey-streaked auburn hair falls in messy waves around her shoulders, giving her a much friendlier look. "Okay, now that we have the messy, business end of things taken care of, let's move on, shall we? The theater is all about releasing your inner spirit in a controlled, premeditated way. If we're going to bring the audience with us into the world of this musical, we need a balance of discipline and unreserved exuberance. You must learn to let go of your inhibitions to fully embrace your character, while staying within the boundaries of your role. And you must know every detail of your character, far beyond the words written in your scripts, or you will never be able to become the part."

Curtis sets down the pile of papers he's been clinging to and steps forward. He straightens his posture, removes his glasses, and lifts his eyes from the floor, instantly morphing from a scared Chihuahua into a take-charge kind of guy. "Even the background characters," he says, "must know who they are. If you're playing a shrinking, shy, flunky to a power-hungry boss, you need to truly believe that your boss will skin you alive for spilling her coffee, or the audience will never believe it. You may not think that anyone will notice you or care about whether you smile or frown while dancing at the ball, but you are all here for a reason." He grins at Mrs. Mason, who curtsies slightly and returns the smile.

"If I hadn't played my part right, none of you would have believed Debbie's act, would you?" Curtis asks. "Often, the background characters will make or break the entire play. Without the supporting cast, the main characters are flat and lifeless, but with the right background, your entire performance comes to life."

Mrs. Mason steps forward again. "Your character is built on the tiny, even insignificant details. A hairstyle. A speech pattern. The way you walk. Even the props you carry will contribute to your persona." She stops pacing and stares down the cheerleader from Northridge. She shakes her head slightly and takes a small sip from her coffee mug.

Suddenly, Mrs. Mason throws the contents of her mug at the cheerleader, who yelps and jumps backward in surprise. But instead of the hot coffee we expected, a flurry of rainbow-colored confetti floats to the floor.

"Remember," Mrs. Mason says, "that in the theater, as in life, things are not always as they appear to be."

Everyone laughs and the cheerleader grins sheepishly. "You scared me," she says. "This is a brand-new sweater. I would've died if I got coffee stains all over it."

"Ah, but I made you believe that my confetti mug was full of hot coffee," Mrs. Mason says. "And that is the point. That is what we're here to do."

She nods, and Curtis passes out pencils. "I want you to use the empty page in the front of your scripts," Mrs. Mason says, "to write out a complete character sketch for your part. Fill in all of the details that are missing from the script. If you don't have a name, give yourself one. Write down your favorite color, the name of your childhood pet, your worst fears. I expect you to know everything about your character. Make it fit the role spelled out in the script, but don't let the written words hold you back. Turn your character into a real person with strengths and weaknesses, hopes and dreams. In twenty minutes, we will break into small groups to introduce ourselves to one another."

She glances at her watch and then back at us. No one moves.

"Well, what are you waiting for? Go!"

I find a quiet spot between the curtain and the stage steps and start writing. "My name is Arika, and I used to be my mother's favorite until she remarried and my perfect, little stepsister stole the spotlight."

"Ugh! I'm totally exhausted." I slump into the passenger seat of Dave's car and kick off my shoes. "If I'm this tired after only our second rehearsal, I seriously doubt I'll make it to opening night. And my feet are freaking killing me. If I have to dance with that uncoordinated Duke Dipweed one more time, I swear, I might murder someone. I think he broke all of my little piggies when he stomped on my foot."

Dave laughs as he slides behind the wheel. He slips the key into the ignition, but doesn't start the engine. "Oh, come on. Nathaniel's a good guy. I think he gets nervous, dancing with you."

I prop my feet up on the dashboard and wiggle my toes. "Well, I think ol' Nate needs more dance lessons or something, because my feet can't take any more of this torture."

"I can help with that."

I shoot him a quizzical look. ""You're going to give him dancing lessons? This I've got to see."

Dave blushes and shakes his head. "No, the other part." He smiles. "Here, give me your feet. I've got the magic touch. I promise, by the time I'm done with you, you'll feel like you were dancing on a cloud all afternoon."

I shift around in my seat until my back is propped against the door and my feet are in his lap.

Dave wasn't kidding about that magical touch. I close my eyes, and in less than five minutes, I've practically melted into a giant puddle of goo.

A sudden, sharp tapping on my window startles me awake, and when I open my eyes, the sun is already starting to set behind the mountains. I sit up sleepily and pull my feet back before turning to look out the window.

Jarod stares at me with his arms crossed and a giant frown on his face.

I roll down the window and smile. "Hey, Jar. What's up?"

"Are you guys having some kind of car trouble?" he asks. "I figured you'd be long gone by now." He glares at Dave and then leans on the window, his face mere inches away from mine. "I can give you a ride home."

Dave smiles. "Nope. We're fine. I was helping Andi with her sore feet, and I guess we kind of lost track of time." There's an edge of challenge in his voice, as if he expects a fight.

"As long as I'm here," Jarod says, "I might as well give you a ride home, Andi. I'm supposed to drop by to see Laina anyway."

Dave reaches across the seat to pat my knee. "Thanks for the offer, but we weren't actually going home yet. Andi and I were going to meet up with some friends for dinner in a bit."

I don't remember making plans, but I nod like some deranged bobble-head doll. Dave and Summer were talking about something at lunch today, when I was busy watching Jarod. I probably said yes without even knowing what I agreed to.

Jarod glances at me and then turns a challenging glare back to Dave. "Are you sure? It's kind of getting late." He reaches through the window and pats my shoulder. "Why don't I just take you home? I don't want you to miss curfew."

I push his hand away. "I think I've got plenty of time, Jar. It's only, um ..."

"It's almost seven. How will you be home for eight

o'clock curfew if you go out now?"

Dave turns the key and revs the engine. "Guess that means we don't have time to waste chatting with you in a parking lot, do we?"

"Besides, I have until eight-thirty," I say. "That's plenty of time to eat."

"Are you sure?" Jarod asks. "You look a little confused."

"I'm not confused, Jar. I'm sleepy." I smile sweetly and pretend not to notice the way he's clenching his jaw. If Jarod has plans with Laina, he can't complain about me spending time with someone else. "Seriously, Dave gives the best foot rubs ever. It totally feels like I've been walking in the clouds all day. I'm so relaxed." I yawn and stretch, arching my back to get the best effect.

I may not have a Barbie doll body, but I know how to use what I've got.

"We were planning to meet up with Emily and Summer and a few other people in a little bit." I can't help smirking a little bit at the way Jarod's staring. If I play this right, he might even decide I'm worth fighting for. "I'd invite you to join us, but you already have plans."

"Well, maybe Laina and I ..." Jarod hesitates.

"Yeah, that's probably not a good idea," I say. "Laina's not really Emily's biggest fan, so she wouldn't want to hang out with us. You can come if you want, but I think you'll have to choose. Me or Laina?"

Jarod gulps and shakes his head. "No, you're right. Laina's expecting me. I should go."

Of course he chooses her. I swallow my frustration, squeeze Dave's hand, and smile innocently at Jarod. "Would you mind letting my parents know that I'll probably be home a little late tonight? We were thinking we might go out to a movie after dinner."

Jarod frowns. "You need to be home before eight-thirty.

Your dad is a 'kill the messenger' kind of guy, and I don't feel like being murdered."

I shrug. If he's choosing Laina, Jarod doesn't get to tell me how to spend my time. Besides, my dad is a giant teddy bear. I don't know why Jarod's always so afraid of him.

"Like you said, it's kind of late already. I don't see how we can do dinner and a movie by then. But don't worry about me." I glance at Dave and then wink at Jarod. "I'll be fine."

"What movie are you going to see? Which theater? What time?"

I giggle and slip into my bubbly voice. "Oh, my gopher, Jarod. Are you stalking me now? I don't think we made definite plans yet. But we might go see that new one with Gertrude McPherson."

"Really?" Jarod asks. "You want to see a thriller about a psychopathic killer that murders her parents and steals her sister's identity?" He shakes his head. "Weren't you the one who slept with a nightlight for a week after we watched *The Hobbit* because Gollum freaked you out?"

I blush. How did he know about the night light? "I loved that movie. And if I get scared, Dave can protect me."

There's no way I'd ever go to see *Sweet, Little Sister*. I don't do scary, and I can't handle gory stuff. Emily's been begging me to see it with her, and it was the first movie I thought about. I don't even know what else is playing. But I'm not about to admit my mistake.

Besides, Dave's smiling and nodding while I ramble on, so either he's playing along, or I really am a terrible friend who forgot all about our plans.

I need to start listening to my own lunchtime conversations.

"So will you tell my parents or not?" I ask. "I only have, like, ten minutes left on my phone, and I don't want to waste them calling home if I don't have to. I'd rather have them available in case I'm ever stranded out in the middle of nowhere with a jerk and need to find a ride home or something."

Jarod's jaw tightens. "I'll tell them." He kicks a loose rock across the parking lot. "But keep your phone on. In case anyone needs you."

"Thanks, Jar. You're the best." I grin and roll up the window before he can answer.

Jarod backs away as Dave pulls out of the parking lot. Part of me wishes he would jump into his car and come racing after us, like he did when Dave gave me a ride home from the diner, but I know he won't. Not tonight.

Not if he already has plans with Laina.

Chapter Twenty

Dave laughs. "Are you sure there's nothing going on between you two? Because I gotta say, from where I'm sitting, that looked like a whole lot of something."

"What? No, of course not. He's in love with my sister, remember? Besides, we … you and me … aren't we kind of …?"

My voice trails off and I realize that I don't exactly know how to classify whatever it is that I've got going on with Dave. We've been spending nearly all of our time together since we went to see *The Phantom of the Opera*. He eats lunch with me and my friends. We've gone out to dinner twice (three times if you count tonight), and he sometimes holds my hand in public. But he's never even tried to kiss me. Not once.

And I suddenly realize I didn't even miss it. If I was falling in like with Dave, I'd miss that, wouldn't I?

"What are we, Andi?" Dave asks. "Since you're always so sure about the status of your relationships, this should be easy for you. What would you call us?"

"I don't know. I guess we're friends?" The word tastes bitter in my mouth, and I turn away to stare out the window. *"Friends"* isn't the right word. But I can't pretend to have feelings I don't.

Dave reaches across the seat and takes my hand, squeezing it quickly before releasing it again with a sigh. "So, buddy, should we call Emily and Summer so they can meet us for dinner, or are you comfortable with the lie you told?"

"What?" I turn to look at him and my heart skips a beat when he flashes that dimpled grin. *I wasn't lying. I do want to be just friends with Dave. I … Oh.*

"We never even made plans to go out tonight, did we?" I ask. "You knew I didn't have a clue, and you let me babble like an idiot."

He laughs. "I thought you'd appreciate a reason not to ride home with that guy. Especially since you're still lusting after him, and he's stringing you along. I was trying to give you an opportunity to cut the strings; I didn't expect you to make up some elaborate story. Didn't anyone ever tell you that you're supposed to keep things vague when you're lying through your teeth?"

I shake my head. "I should have left the lying to the expert."

"Nah." Dave grins. "You're pretty good at it. Natural talent and all."

"And here I was, feeling like a terrible person because I thought you, Emily and Summer made plans while I wasn't paying attention."

"Yeah, I noticed your distraction at lunch." He frowns. "You know, for someone who doesn't mean anything to you, Jarod sure takes up a lot of your attention."

I blush. "Is it really that obvious?" No one else ever sees through my act, but it's almost like Dave can read my mind.

"It's only obvious if you know what to watch for." He smirks. "What can I say? I notice."

A heavy silence hangs in the air between us, and I desperately want to fill it, but I don't know what to say. I clear my throat, preparing to apologize, but before I can speak, Dave flips on the radio and tosses me his cell phone.

"You want to call Emily and Summer? Tell them to meet us at the Spaghetti Bowl in fifteen minutes. We can skip the movie, but if we don't get your friends to meet us for dinner, or at least dessert, you're going to crack when Jarod asks you about it later. We might as well avoid the drama now."

I grin and punch in Summer's number. Not that I really need an alibi. Jarod won't bother to ask about our night, and it's not like I can't keep a secret. But things will definitely be less awkward with Dave if I have my friends along for backup.

I can worry about defining our relationship later.

Emily hands her menu to the waitress and then bounces excitedly in her seat. "You have to see the dress I got," she squeals, pulling a large shopping bag from under the table. She drapes a handful of royal blue satin across her arm and grins. "Isn't this the most gorgeous color you've ever seen? And wait 'til you see the whole dress. I look amazing. Matthew will totally flip."

She starts to pull the dress out of the bag, but Summer stops her. "There's no room for a fashion show in the Spaghetti Bowl, Em."

Emily smiles sheepishly and tucks her dress back into

the bag. "You're right. It may have spaghetti straps, but I'd hate to get sauce on that thing."

Dave groans and tosses a breadstick across the table. "That was terrible."

"You only wish you could be this awesome," Emily says. She slides her bag back under the table and grins. "Summer and I convinced the guys they should go in together to rent a limo. You guys want to join us?"

"Actually," Dave says, "I've already got plans. Sorry." He glances at me and then digs into the plate of spaghetti the waitress sets in front of him.

I smile and attack my plate of fettuccini. I wonder what fabulous plans he has up his sleeve.

"Do you have a date for prom yet?" Nick grins at me with a bashful, puppy dog look on his face and leans against my locker.

I push him out of the way so I can grab my books. "I'm skipping prom. And you can quit the puppy dog pout. It doesn't work on me, remember?"

I thought Dave and I were going together, but when I asked him about our prom plans last night, he said he was going with a group of his friends.

He didn't even invite me to join them.

"You can't skip it," Nick says, falling into step beside me as I walk away. "This is supposed to be the best night of our lives. You don't want to go through the rest of your life wondering about what you missed out on, do you?"

"I don't need to wonder. I've already been there and done that. Three times."

"You're worried about finding the perfect date, right?" He grins and slings one arm across my shoulders. "Well, today is your lucky day, because I don't have a date yet either. We can go together, and we'll be the hottest couple there for the second year in a row."

Nick and I do look good together. But that's not the point.

"I'm not doing it this year. All that time and money spent on hair and makeup and a dress, and all you have to show for it is a cheesy, awkward picture with a date you probably won't even be talking to by this time next year. No thanks."

Nick leans against a bank of lockers and smiles, stretching casually so that he can flex his muscles without being all obvious about it. His tight t-shirt stretches across his stomach, highlighting perfect, washboard abs that totally make me want to reach out and touch him. I know that ploy too, but that doesn't make it any less delicious.

"Which is why you should go with me. We had fun last year, and here we are. Talking."

I laugh. "Tempting. But my answer's still no."

"So is this an objection to the idea of prom itself, as in the actual dance, or are you trying to let me down easy so you can keep your options open in case someone better comes along?"

"No waiting for a better offer or any other offer. I'm just not doing prom this year."

Nick flexes his muscles again with another not-so-casual stretch. "Then what are we doing instead? And does this mean I don't have to rent a tux and a limo?"

"What about bowling? Tux is optional, but I want a limo." I can have fun without Dave.

"It's a date." Nick smiles and saunters away.

"Andi!" Emily squeals, running up and practically tackling me with a massive hug. "Why didn't you tell me that you and Nick were getting together again?" She steps back and bounces a few times. "You guys are so freaking cute. Now we can triple date with Summer and Josh." She gasps. "We have to go shopping after school today. Summer and I saw the perfect prom dress for you when we were picking up our own dresses last week, and it's still on sale."

"Wow. What did I miss?" Summer asks, hurrying to catch up with us.

Emily bubbles over about Nick and me again, and I literally have to put my hand over her mouth to get her to shut up. "We're going bowling," I say. "No prom."

Emily waves her hand dismissively. "Oh, please. Bowling is just the appetizer. That's where it all begins. You'll go out tonight, and then you'll hang out a few times over spring break. You're totally going to change your mind about prom, so don't leave your dress shopping for the last minute. That's when desperate girls get stuck with the most disgusting things." She shudders. "We're already cutting it close. We only have two more weeks."

I laugh and grab Emily's arm, steering her outside and through the parking lot to Summer's car. "I hate to break it to ya, Em, but I can't go shopping today. You're dropping me off at rehearsal, remember? And I'm not bowling with Nick tonight. I probably won't even see him again until after spring break. We're going bowling on prom night. Instead of the dance. So I don't need a dress, even if it is on sale."

Chapter Twenty-One

I groan and roll over, knocking my alarm clock to the floor, and pulling my blankets up over my head. Spring break is supposed to be for sleeping in and then staying up late to party. But we've had extra choreography rehearsals for *Cinderella* every night this week, and now Curtis expects us to be at the theater by nine o'clock in the morning on the last Saturday of spring break for a full-day practice session. Because Duke Dipweed still can't get the choreography right.

I must have been insane to let Dave and Jarod talk me into this.

I hear my bedroom door creak open, and I pull the blankets tighter, snuggling down into my mattress. "Leave me alone," I mutter. "I'm exhausted, and my feet hurt. They can rehearse without me."

I shouldn't have let Laina see my rehearsal schedule. Barbie dolls don't get tired, and Miss Perfect's still determined to turn me into a younger version of herself.

I wrap myself up like a blanket burrito, resisting the sharp tug from my enemy. Luckily, I'm stronger than Laina, even when I'm sleep-deprived. She'll give up soon, and then I can rest in peace.

Eventually, the pulling stops, and I hear retreating footsteps. But when I relax, someone grabs me by the waist and lifts me out of bed, blanket cocoon and all.

"Time to get up, sleepyhead," Dave says. "We're already running late, and you don't want to keep Prince Charming waiting, do you?"

There's a hint of a challenge in his voice, but by the time I manage to pull the blankets away from my face to look at him, there's no trace of bitterness in his eyes. Just the mischievous twinkle I've missed so much lately.

He tightens his hold on me for a quick hug, and then he drops me on my butt in the middle of my bedroom floor, yanking my blankets away in one quick motion, like that cool magician trick where they pull a tablecloth off a table and leave all the dishes in place.

Except yanking the warm blankets off a sleepy girl is so much less cool.

Dave tosses them onto my bed, and then he turns to look at me. I blush as his eyes slowly travel the length of my body, and I wish I'd chosen my fuzzy, flannel pajamas to sleep in last night, instead of my sports bra and a pair of boxers.

I jump up and glare at him, hands on my hips. "Well?" I ask. "Are you at least going to let me get dressed, or do I have to go to rehearsal in this?"

Dave smirks. "I like what you're wearing right now, but we wouldn't want to give poor Prince Charming a heart attack, now would we?" He laughs. "You have three minutes to get dressed, or I'm coming back in here. And I will carry you out of the house in that lovely outfit, if I have to. So don't even think about going back to bed." He grabs the hair brush from my nightstand and tosses it to me. "And you might want to do something with your hair."

A quick glance in the mirror confirms that I'm rocking a total bed head. My hair is completely mashed flat on one side and sticking out at all angles on the other. Perfect.

"Well, if you're only going to give me three minutes, then get out, because natural beauty like mine usually takes at least three and a half." I grab my pillow from the floor and hurl it at his retreating back.

As soon as the door clicks shut behind him, I race to the closet and grab my hot pink sweats and a grey t-shirt that says "I'm Not Really Wicked, I Just Act That Way" across the front in large, shiny, hot pink letters. I pull my clothes on and grab clean socks out of my drawer. Then, I dig my grey sneakers out of my closet and toss them, with my socks, the hair brush, and a couple of hairbands, into a bag. Dropping the bag on my bed on the way past, I run to the bathroom to wash my face and brush my teeth.

I still have foam all over my lips and a toothbrush sticking out of my mouth when the bathroom door swings open.

"Dave!" I spit and quickly rinse my mouth. "Oh, my gorgonzola, I'm in the bathroom! Hello? Boundaries, please."

He arches one eyebrow. "If you weren't decent, you would have locked the door. I've seen teeth before. Yours aren't that shocking." He grabs me around the waist and tosses me over his shoulder, carrying me out of the bathroom and through my bedroom. "You've had three minutes. Time's up," he says.

"Wait! My shoes." I point to the bag on the end of my bed and kick my feet. He grabs it and carries me down the hall. Laina sits in the living room, laughing at me, and she doesn't lift a finger to help as Dave carries me outside. I shiver as soon as we hit the cool morning air. "Seriously? I don't even get to grab my coat?"

Dave sighs and turns back toward the house.

Laina meets us at the door with my jacket in one hand and a breakfast burrito in the other. "Thanks, traitor," I say, snatching them both from her. "I'm so getting even for this."

She laughs. "I guess you shouldn't have stayed up so late talking to Nick last night. You knew you had play practice this morning."

She is so dead to me.

I stuff my feet into my socks and sneakers as Dave pulls away from the house. Then, I brush my hair and twist it up into a neat bun.

When my stomach grumbles, I remember the breakfast burrito and take a giant bite. Laina managed to put together the perfect ratio of eggs and cheese, with just enough salsa for flavor, but not enough that it's likely to drip and ruin my outfit. Not that the perfect burrito is enough to make me forgive her, but it's a start. At least I won't starve my way through the morning.

"You went out with Nick last night?"

I can hear the forced casualness in Dave's voice, and I know he's dying to pump me for more information. But I'm not about to give him the satisfaction. I smile and take another bite. After the way he barged in on me, he doesn't deserve to hear the details. Besides, we didn't even go out. Nick called and we talked for, like, ten minutes about our non-prom plans.

"Must've been a heck of a night, if you couldn't even manage to drag your butt out of bed this morning." His smile is totally forced, and there's no mistaking the angry edge to his voice.

"So? It's not like my social life has anything to do with you." He doesn't have any right to be jealous. We're not together and if he was at all interested, he would have asked me to prom, instead of blowing me off for his friends.

"I'm just saying, you shouldn't have agreed to be in the

play if you're not going to take it seriously. There are a lot of people counting on you."

"Ugh. What's your deal today? You know I've been working my butt off for this play." I point to the clock in the dashboard. "It's only eight thirty-five, and I know it doesn't take twenty-five minutes to get to the theater. Especially not on a Saturday morning, when anyone with half a brain is still in bed. Is there some special reason that we need to be there so freaking early?"

"I didn't want to be late."

"As if we've ever been late to a single rehearsal. I bet Mrs. Mason isn't even there yet, and we'll have to sit in an empty parking lot until she shows up." I take another bite of my burrito and glare at him while I chew. "I totally had time to take a shower and do my makeup. And to find something decent to wear. I didn't even get to grab my lunch before you so rudely carried me out of the house, and now I'm going to starve to death halfway through the day."

"No problem. I'll take you out." Dave shakes his head. "And I happen to recall a certain someone explaining to me last week that she always takes her shower at night before going to bed, so that she can have extra time to sleep in. I didn't make you miss a thing."

"Okay, so maybe I didn't need to shower, but what about my makeup? What about my outfit? You didn't even give me time to brush my hair."

"You brushed it in the car," he says. "And you would have worn it in a bun anyway. You always do for rehearsals."

I look out the window. "I look like a total slob."

Dave pulls into the totally empty parking lot and into a space next to the door. He turns off the car and slides around in his seat until he's facing me. "I think you're beautiful. Even in sweats and a t-shirt, and with no makeup." His lips curl up into the same smug, little smirk he wore when he pulled me out of bed and dumped me on my butt. "If he needs the makeup and fancy, designer clothes to see how beautiful you are, then maybe you deserve something a little better than a charming prince."

"Seriously?" I shake my head. "How many times do I have to tell you that there's nothing going on between us? Jarod and I are not together. We're friends. I have tons of friends, and I talk to at least one of them every single day. So you can drop the jealous boyfriend act. Because, guess what, Dave? You're not my boyfriend either."

Mrs. Mason pulls into the parking lot, and I jump out of the car to follow her into the theater. I can hear Dave scrambling after me, but I don't have time for jealous, wannabe boyfriends. I have an intense choreography rehearsal that's supposed to start in less than fifteen minutes.

By the time we break for lunch, I'm starving, and all I can think of is the delicious food I so carefully packed last night before I went to bed. A turkey, bacon and avocado sandwich, pita chips and hummus, cheese puffs, celery sticks, chocolate-covered jelly beans, a bottle of flavored water and a giant bag of Oreos ... all packed neatly into the Disney Princesses lunch bag I used to take to school when I was little. And it's still sitting on the top shelf of my refrigerator, all cold and lonely.

Dave waves at me from backstage, but I pretend not to see him. He thinks Jarod will only notice me if I'm all perfect and beautiful, but he's wrong, and I'm going to prove it.

I saunter over to where Jarod is chatting with the duke and Cinderella.

"Hey, Jar. What's up?"

He smiles and pulls me into a giant hug. "Hi,

gorgeous."

Take that, Dave!

Jarod doesn't even care about my sloppy old sweats. "Hi, yourself." I smile and resist the urge to look over my shoulder to make sure Dave is watching.

"Nathaniel and I were gonna go get some lunch from the deli across the street," Jarod says. He glances at Cinderella. "Cara thinks she's too good for us, but you'll join us, won't you?" He pauses and looks over my shoulder. "Or do you already have plans with your little friend?"

"Nope. I'm totally free." I frown. "But I'm skipping lunch today. I'm not that hungry."

Jarod laughs. "You're never 'not that hungry.' You're the only girl I've ever met who knows she's sexy, even when eating like a real person. Come on. It'll be fun."

"Well, I accidentally left my purse at home this morning, so I don't have any money."

Jarod's eyes light up. "Maybe Laina could bring it to you. She might even want to come out with us."

"She's busy," I say, not even bothering to fake a smile.

"No problem," Nathaniel says. "I'll take care of you. You can pay me back later."

"Nah, I've got her," Jarod says, grabbing my hand and pulling me away. As we walk past Dave, I catch a hint of a smug smirk on Jarod's lips.

Because boys will turn anything into a competition. Even dating.

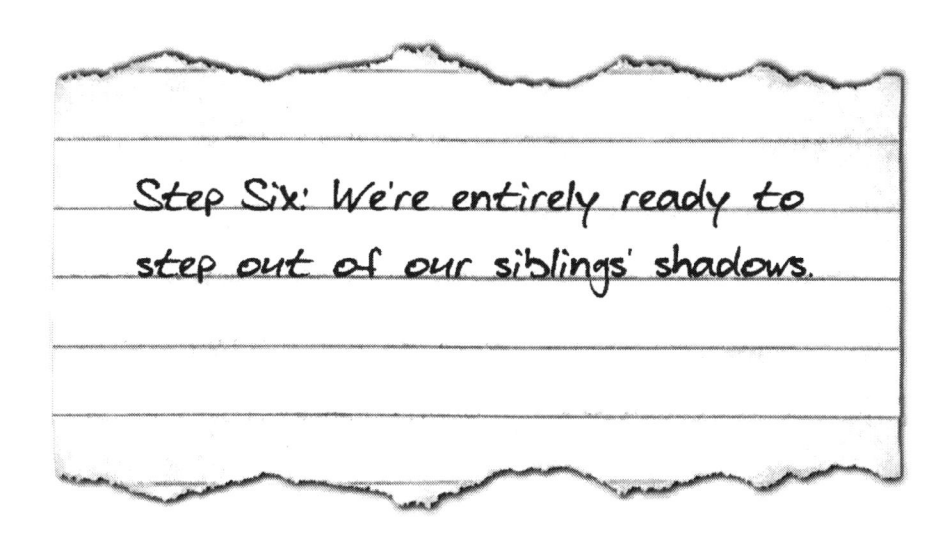

Step Six: We're entirely ready to step out of our siblings' shadows.

Chapter Twenty-Two

I weave a spray of miniature pink silk roses into Laina's hair and step back to admire my handiwork. A dab of glittery lip gloss and a hint of mascara, and she's ready for the prom.

Almost.

I confiscate her bulky purse and dump it out onto the bed. From the pile of miscellaneous junk, I select two sticks of gum, a twenty-dollar bill, a pen, and a small notepad, and I slip them into my tiny, black, beaded clutch. Then, I toss in my lip gloss, just in case.

"What's wrong with the purse I have?"

"Well, for starters, it's huge and clunky and that paisley print totally clashes with your dress."

"How does anything clash with black?"

I laugh and hand her the clutch. "Trust me. That monstrosity clashes with everything. Besides, you don't want to carry something that huge all night."

"But this little thing doesn't even fit my diary." She

reaches for the pile of stuff on the bed, but I step in front of her to block the grab.

"If you have time to write in your diary while you're at the prom, you're doing it wrong."

"I couldn't even get a date. I'm obviously doing it wrong." Laina glances at her reflection and wraps her arms around her waist. "What if I'm stuck sitting by myself all night?" Her usually confident smile droops and her shoulders slump. "No one's going to want to dance with me. I should have listened to Kendra. This dress makes me look fat, doesn't it? Maybe I should wear the one I got for Uncle Herbert's funeral?"

She yanks open her closet door and starts digging through the hangers in the back. I sigh and pull the shapeless funeral dress out of her hands. "You look gorgeous. Now stop worrying. Shane's gonna kick himself for passing up a chance with you."

I grab her gauzy, black wrap and toss it around her shoulders. "Come on. Mom and Dad want to take some pictures of you all dressed up before you go, and you're kind of running late. The Witch won't like it if you keep her waiting."

Laina throws one last, longing look at the pile of crap on her bed and then looks at the beaded clutch in her hand. I laugh and push her down the hall to the living room, where Mom and Dad are waiting with the camera.

"Oh," Mom gasps. "You're so beautiful." She grabs Laina's hand and twirls her around to inspect the dress from all angles.

"You look like Cinderella, on her way to the ball," Dad says.

Yeah, except Laina's not-so-charming prince decided to choose someone else, and she's stuck with the Wicked Witch for a date.

"Are you sure you don't want to go bowling with Nick

and me?" I ask.

Laina shakes her head. "I'm not exactly dressed for bowling, and I'm not going to get the last three hours of my life back. I'm already all fancy, so I might as well go. Besides, Kendra is counting on me." She shrugs.

"I still don't understand why you're going with her instead of Rob," I say. "You could've had the whole cliché prom experience."

Laina cringes. "Rob wasn't really interested in me." She studies her perfectly-manicured nails and swallows hard. She looks up at me and smiles, but her eyes flash with that terrified child look again before she slips back into her plastic Barbie façade. "Besides, I couldn't let Kendra go alone." She fidgets and glances at her reflection in the large mirror above the fireplace. Her fingers flutter to the lace trim at her neckline, and she straightens her skirt.

I should have known she'd think Rob asked her to make me jealous when I said no, even though it was totally the other way around. Maybe I should have pointed out the way he kept ogling the whole time he was talking to me.

"Well, you look beautiful, dear," Mom says. "And I'm proud of you for standing by your friend." She holds up the camera and smiles. "Are you ready?"

Laina poses stiffly while Mom snaps a zillion pictures. Even though Mom keeps telling her to smile, she looks like she did when I asked her about Anthony after reading her diary. With each snap of the camera, Laina's mask of perfection cracks and crumbles away. Something's wrong with my sister, but I can't exactly ask her about it with Mom acting like the paparazzi. And I haven't exactly been successful in getting Laina to open up lately.

Dad catches my eye and nods subtly toward Laina, silently begging me to fix my sister's waning self-esteem.

"Let's get some pictures of the two of us together." I say. I jump across the room and grab Laina's hand, catching her off-guard and spinning her around. I strike a nineteen-seventies disco pose and plaster my goofiest grin across my face. Laina laughs, like I knew she would, and her worried look wavers.

Mom, still totally oblivious, frowns and lowers the camera. "Andi, this is a big night for your sister. Can't you let her have this moment without jumping in?"

Laina clutches her wrap, pulling it around her body, as if she's trying to hide inside it. Dad nods at me again and raises his eyebrows.

He sees it, too.

"Sorry, Mom," I say. "You have enough serious pictures. It's time for the outtakes."

I spin Laina around, pulling her wrap from her shoulders and contort my face into the craziest grimace I can manage.

Mom sighs and glances helplessly from me to the camera to Dad.

I waltz Laina around the room and then dip her deeply, holding the pose until Mom finally relents and starts snapping pictures again. Laina giggles hesitantly.

Dad slips out of the room and returns a moment later, dragging Nick behind him. He shoots me a questioning glance and then whispers something to Nick before turning to Mom and Laina with a smile.

"Look what I found on the doorstep. It's a little lost puppy. What do you think, girls? Should we keep him or send him away?"

I giggle and nod, but Laina stops mid-twirl and gulps. The blood drains from her face, leaving her white as a ghost. Her eyes widen, and she takes a step backward, grabbing her wrap from the floor and pulling it tight around her shoulders. I'm not sure what Dad has in mind, but I'm not sure if it will work. Laina doesn't let most people see her silly side. Especially not people as gorgeous as Nick.

Dad claps Nick on the back and nods. "Looks like you have my daughter's approval," he says. "I guess we'll keep you."

Nick inhales sharply and puts his hand over his heart. "Wow. You're beautiful. I think you literally took my breath away."

Dad grins and crosses the room to slip an arm around Mom. "Yessiree," he says. "Our little Andi is quite the looker, isn't she?" He winks at me and shakes his head, reminding me to play along with whatever plan he has up his sleeve.

Laina glances at her reflection again. She frowns and takes another step back, as if she's trying to hide behind me.

Nick smiles and takes a step forward. "Andi is very pretty. No doubt about it."

He crosses the room in three giant steps. "But I was actually talking about your other daughter, sir." He winks at me, and I catch a brief look between Nick and my dad.

Nick takes Laina's hand, kisses it, and bows slightly. Then, he looks at her with a flirtatious twinkle in his eyes. "I think I asked the wrong sister to go out with me tonight," he says. "You're a goddess."

I have to bite my lip hard to suppress the giggles that threaten to escape. I've heard Nick use some really cheesy lines, but this one is the worst.

Laina blushes and pulls her hand away. "I'm a regular, ol' mortal girl," she says. "There's nothing special about me." She steals another quick glance at her reflection. This time, though, her chin lifts slightly and her spine straightens.

I guess it's true what they say. Flattery totally works. And Nick is a master. He's managed to turn a super-cheesy, borderline-creepy compliment into what appears to be sincere admiration. Instead of leering at Laina's Barbie doll figure, he stares dreamily into her eyes, as if he can see straight into her soul. And Laina's totally eating it up.

Nick's like a super-hot fairy godfather, changing

Cinderella's ragged self-esteem into a beautiful ego made of awesome.

He leans in and whispers loud enough for everyone to hear, "Will you marry me?"

Laina giggles. "Stop it, Nick. Andi's going to think you're serious."

He grins and slips an arm around her waist. "What if I am? Come on. I've got a limo parked right outside. If we leave now, we can make it to Vegas by morning."

She blushes, shaking her head slowly, unable to speak.

Dad grabs the camera from Mom, who is staring open-mouthed at the scene, and he starts snapping pictures of the two of them. Laina cringes and ducks her head, but Nick struts and hams it up, pulling her into pose after silly pose until she's laughing and clowning right along with him.

I've got to admit, they make a really cute couple.

Normally, this is the type of thing that makes my blood boil. The constant reminders that I will never be enough to measure up against the impossible standard Laina sets are usually enough to make me want to cry secret tears. But Nick is so perfectly repairing the damage I caused with my stupid question that I can't actually hold it against him.

Laina grabs my arm and pulls me over to pose with her and Nick, and we spend the next few minutes trying to come up with the silliest prom pictures in history.

Finally, Dad lowers the camera and looks at Nick. "Well, son," he says, "I'd say you have a choice to make. Are you going to do the honorable thing and keep your date with my beautiful Andrea, as you promised? Or are you going to prove yourself a rogue and attempt to steal away her sister?"

Nick grins and slips his arms around Laina's waist. "What do you say, baby? Want to run away with me? I'm sure little sis will get over the heartbreak eventually."

Laina laughs and spins out of Nick's arms. "Sorry," she says, "but I already have a date tonight." She glances at her watch. "And I'm seriously late." She crosses the room and kisses Dad on the cheek, and then she hugs Mom, who is still gaping at Nick.

"I'll see you all later," she says. "Oh, and Andi? You might want to reconsider your plans tonight. I think your date is kind of a player." She grabs her keys and the little, beaded clutch I gave her, and then she skips out the door.

"Well played, son," Dad says. "You should consider a career in acting." He kisses Mom on the cheek and laughs. "Although I think this one was nearly ready to skin you alive. She's like a mama bear when it comes to protecting her daughters. Generally, I'd advise you not to mess with her cubs."

Mom elbows Dad in the ribs, and glares between him and Nick. "And what, exactly, was this little performance supposed to accomplish?" she demands. "Did either of you ever stop to consider Andi's feelings? How she would feel when her date started openly flirting with her sister? And what if Alaina had called your bluff? Were you prepared for the consequences?"

Dad stumbles backward and collapses on the couch, clutching his side as if Mom seriously wounded him. When Mom doesn't crack a smile, he jumps back up and wraps his arms around her. "Don't worry, sugarplum. We've got a couple of smart girls. If Laina thought for one minute that Nick was truly serious, she never would have skipped out of here like she did." He nods at me. "And our little actress knows a con job when she sees one."

Mom frowns. "I still say it wasn't right. How will Laina be able to trust any of you after this?" She glares at Nick. "And you. How dare you?"

I laugh and shake my head, adopting Mom's frown and crossing my arms. "Shame on you, Nick. Playing with my heart and toying with Laina's emotions."

Nick grins. "Who says I was playing? You've seen your

sister, right? She's totally hot." His gaze travels slowly up and down my body, appraisingly, lingering long enough to make me blush. "But I guess you'll do."

I laugh. "See, the problem is that you're comparing Laina's formal wear with my casual look. Just wait until I finish getting ready. Then, you'll see who's the hot one."

I dash out of the room and run down the hall to my parents' bedroom, where I grab Dad's old bowling shirt out of his closet and throw it on over my tank top. I pull my hair up into a sloppy side ponytail, and then I rummage through Mom's makeup drawer to find a bright blue eye shadow that went out of style in the late eighties. I slather it on my eyelids and paint my lips with a bright red lipstick that Mom bought by mistake and forgot to take back to the store.

I stroll back to the living room and twirl slowly in my custom prom night outfit. "Who's the sexy sister now?"

Nick grins and clasps both hands over his heart. "Clearly, I made the right choice. You are breathtaking."

"Technically, Laina made the choice for you," I say, "but I'll accept that answer. Come on, Casanova. Let's go."

"So … Vegas, right?"

I grab my jacket and my purse. "Sure. As long as you can get me home by curfew."

Dad laughs, and Mom finally smiles. "I suppose, if you're going all the way to Vegas, you can stay out an extra half hour. Be home by midnight."

"Seriously? You told Laina to be home by two. And I have to be home at midnight?"

"Well, she's going all the way to prom at the Candlelight Inn across town," Dad says, chuckling, "and you're only going to Vegas. It seems fair to me."

"We already discussed this, sweetie," Mom says. "The bowling alley closes at eleven. There's really no reason for you to stay out past midnight. Whereas the prom isn't over until twelve, and Laina wanted to go to that little get together afterward."

I grab my jacket and shove my arms into the sleeves. "Whatever." I take Nick's hand and stomp out into the cool evening air.

Chapter Twenty-Three

After scrubbing the flashback-from-the-eighties makeup off of my face, I step out of the shower and slip into my fuzzy, flannel pajamas. I brush the tangles out of my wet hair and weave it into a tight braid.

Even with the unfair curfew, this was the best prom night ever. I threw about a zillion gutter balls, but I actually got a strike after Nick convinced the bowling alley manager to put up the kiddie bumpers for me. It was so much better than performing for a bunch of prom zombies.

And Nick was a perfect break from all the boy drama and relationship pressure.

I toss Dad's bowling shirt into the hamper on my way out of the bathroom, and then I grin at my reflection in my dresser mirror and slip my feet into my furry slippers. I totally deserve a midnight snack.

Mom and Dad went to bed right after Nick dropped me off and I gave them a condensed report of my night, but I can hear the muffled sounds of the TV from their bedroom.

They're waiting up for Laina to check in when she gets home. Mom swears that neither of them can rest until both of their children are home and accounted for, but I suspect Dad would totally go to sleep if she let him.

I slip down the quiet hallway to the kitchen, where I pour a giant glass of milk and toss a stack of Oreo cookies onto a plate. The perfect snack to end the perfect day.

But as I twist open the first cookie, a sharp knock on the door shatters the stillness.

Jarod stands on the porch, his bowtie hanging limply around his neck. His tuxedo jacket has some kind of strange smudge on the left shoulder, and his hair sticks out at odd angles, the way it does when he's been nervously raking his fingers through it.

"Can we talk?"

"Sure. Come on in." I step back and open the door wide to let him through.

Jarod glances over his shoulder at the empty street, and then at my pajamas. He blushes slightly, and then he clears his throat. "I know you're ready for bed, but I was hoping that maybe we could talk privately." He glances over his shoulder again, as if he's expecting someone to magically materialize on the porch steps behind him.

"Laina and the Witch were going to go to Pete's after party, if that's what you're worried about," I say. "She probably won't be home for a while."

He nods and slips inside. "I guess she'll probably still do that. I think they're fighting, but Laina wouldn't cancel plans."

I shake my head and walk back to the kitchen. I pour another glass of milk, push my plate of cookies to the middle of the table, and sit beside Jarod. "What's up? No offense, but you look kind of terrible."

"I feel kind of terrible." He picks up a cookie and twists it open, but instead of eating it, he stares at the crème filling as if it holds all the answers to life, the universe, and everything else.

"So?" I dunk a cookie and take a bite. "You wanna tell me what's going on?"

"She chose Shane. I lost." He looks up, and when his eyes meet mine, he blushes. "I guess you're probably the last person on earth who wants to hear me complaining about this."

I roll my eyes.

"But now it's over. She's made her decision, and there's nothing to come between us." He brushes a stray hair out of my face and caresses my cheek.

I close my eyes and allow the electricity of his touch course through my body for a moment before I pull away. "Why are you here, Jarod?"

He slides closer and takes my hand. "I told you. Laina chose Shane. You should've seen the way her eyes lit up when he asked her to dance. He's obviously the one she wants. I'll never be anything but a friend, and it's time I accepted that. She's made her choice."

I squeeze his hand and take a deep breath before pulling away. "But why are you here?"

His brow furrows. "Aren't you even listening? Laina made her choice, and it wasn't me."

He reaches across the table, but I stand up before he can touch me. I step away, putting space between us, and take a slow, deep breath as I clench and unclench my hands. When I have my emotions under control, I try again. "Yes, I hear you. But do you hear yourself?" I lean against the sink. "Laina made her choice. Fine. But why are you here? With me?"

He stands and gathers me into his arms. "Isn't it obvious? Now we can be together." He nibbles my bottom lip playfully. "There's nothing to come between us anymore." He traces my cheek with soft kisses and then tightens his arms around me as his lips find mine.

I groan and turn my head, summoning all of my willpower to push him away. "But have you made your choice?" My heart is racing, and I want nothing more than to melt into him. I've been dreaming of this moment for years, but this isn't how I imagined it. I want him to want me first. I want to be the one he daydreams about. The one he comes looking for when everything is going right, and not just when he needs an ego-boost.

"I don't understand." Jarod cups my cheek in his hand and leans in for another kiss. "What choice is left for me to make?"

I squirm out of his arms, holding up my hands to keep a safe distance between us. "Stop, Jar. I can't think clearly when you do that."

"Maybe we've both been thinking too much."

I step away, increasing the distance between us. "I'm serious. I won't be your rebound girl. I deserve more than to be the one you turn to when you can't have what you really want."

"What if you're the one I really want?"

"Answer one question." I take a deep breath and hold it for a moment before I let it go. "What if Laina came home right now and said she'd made a mistake? What if she realized that she really wants you? She chose Shane, but are you ready to choose me?"

Jarod lowers his eyes. "That's more than one question."

"And I think you just answered them all."

He takes my hand and looks into my eyes. "That's not fair. How am I supposed to know what might happen? I've been in love with Laina for years, but this." He waves his hand to indicate the space between us. "This is all new to me."

"Jarod, I've been here all along."

"But that's different. We're friends. I didn't expect to fall for you."

I sigh. "Why were you so worried that Laina might

come home and catch us talking?"

He drops my hand and sits at the table. His right shoulder lifts in a slow, half-shrug, and he stares into his still-full glass of milk.

"Is that question too hard? How about this one: Are you willing to stay with me until Laina comes home, so you can tell her that we're together?"

He doesn't look at me.

I take another deep breath, fighting to keep my voice even. "Have you told any of your friends how you feel about me? Are you willing to be with me in public, instead of stealing kisses when no one is looking?"

He raises his head, finally meeting my gaze. "I don't know. Can't we see where this all goes before—"

"No, Jar, we can't!" My voice comes out stronger and louder than I'd intended, and I pause, waiting to see if Mom or Dad will come check on me. When they don't appear, I sit at the table across from Jarod. I flatten my hands on the cold, wooden surface, gathering strength from the physical barrier between us.

"I don't want to be the consolation prize. If I'm not your first choice, I don't want to be chosen." I want someone whose eyes light up when I walk into the room. Someone who thinks I'm the blue ribbon. My mind flashes on a pair of rich, chocolate-brown eyes and a smile with an adorable dimple that always makes my stomach flutter.

"Andi—"

Jarod reaches for my hands, but I pull away. "Good night, Jarod. Please turn off the light and lock the door when you leave." I turn and walk out of the kitchen, without waiting for him to respond.

I get to school early Monday morning and wait for Dave at his locker. We've been avoiding each other since I ditched him at rehearsal a week ago, but I couldn't stop thinking about him yesterday, and I'm sure he's missing me, too.

Dave offers me a half-hearted, dimple-less smile as he twirls the combination on his lock, but he doesn't speak. I clear my throat and take a deep breath, reminding myself not to be nervous. It's just Dave.

"So Jarod came over after prom on Saturday night," I say. "I guess Laina and Shane got together at the dance, and so he was feeling lonely."

Dave's jaw clenches and he yanks a stack of books out of his locker before slamming the door and whirling around to face me. "Can't you talk to Emily or Summer about this?" he asks. "I'm not really in the mood for a play-by-play of how you and Jarod hooked up."

He stalks off down the hall, and I scurry to catch up, grabbing his arm just as we reach the door to first period. "Dave, I told him no. I don't want to be his back-up girlfriend." I stare into Dave's eyes, silently pleading with him to read my mind, the way he's always done before. "I think I'm falling for someone else."

He sighs. "Can we talk about this later, when we're not almost late for class? I'll find you at lunch." And he disappears into the classroom without waiting for my response.

Emily bounces up to me as the warning bell rings, bubbling over with excitement. She says something about prom and Matthew and her dress. I hear enough to realize that the night went well for her, but I'm only half listening. I keep stealing glances across the room, trying to catch Dave watching me.

He doesn't look up from his notebook even once.

Chapter Twenty-Four

Summer waves her hand in front of my face and snaps her fingers impatiently.

I look up from the mound of soggy fries I've been rearranging on my lunch tray. "Sorry, what did I miss?"

She glances at my tray. "You haven't even touched your corndog. Since when do you pass up fried foods?"

I try to smile, but I can't keep up the act today. "Just tired, I guess."

She points across the cafeteria at Dave, who is walking slowly toward us, balancing his lunch tray on a tall stack of books. "You sure you're not still upset about a certain someone who didn't ask you to the prom?"

My heart skips a beat, but I'm not about to admit anything until I know how he feels. "Nope. Just didn't sleep well last night."

I sit up straight, running my fingers through my hair to smooth the frizz. I arch my back slightly and hold my breath to accent my barely-there curves, and then I glance at Jarod to see if he's watching.

He is.

Dave stops mid-step, his smile fading as he looks at me, then at Jarod and back at me. He dumps his lunch tray into the trash and stomps out of the cafeteria. I consider going after him, but Summer is staring at me like she's trying to figure out one of life's great mysteries. And I don't have the energy to explain it all now.

Emily drops her tray onto the table and sits down beside Summer. Then she turns to kiss Pete, who slides onto the bench beside her.

"Wait, what am I missing?" I ask. "Since when are you two together?"

Summer laughs. "See? This is exactly what I was talking about. It's like you're on another planet or something."

I glance at the cafeteria doors, through which Dave disappeared. She's not far off.

Emily smiles and leans against Pete, who plants tiny kisses on her cheeks and forehead in between bites. "I told you the whole story before first period. Weren't you listening?"

I shake my head and frown.

She sighs. "Long story short, Matthew's a creep. I was stranded, and Pete saved me."

"Wow. I skip one little dance, and I miss out on all the drama."

"Speaking of drama," Summer says, leaning across the table with wide eyes, "what's the deal with your sister and Shane Crawford? I want all the juicy details."

I lean forward. "What do you mean? I didn't hear about any drama."

After Jarod's visit Saturday night, I'd expected Laina to come bouncing into my room when she came home, to tell me about Shane, but she went straight to bed. And then she totally avoided me yesterday, hiding out in her room with the door locked. She even managed to convince Mom and Dad that she was too sick to go to church, and they let her stay home, even though Mom thinks skipping church is practically one of the seven deadly sins.

"So what happened?" I ask.

Pete laughs. "I tried to tell Shane he was wasting his time, but he said he had to prove that he was choosing her over Rachel or something. So he wrote that song."

Emily grins. "I wish someone would write a song for me."

Pete wraps his arms around her waist and nuzzles her neck. "I'm not much of a writer, but I'll sing one for you."

"Ugh! Get a room," Summer says.

I pop a fry into my mouth and grin. It's kind of nice to see Emily this happy. "Okay, someone fill me in on the details, because Laina didn't tell me anything."

Emily slips into gossip mode, leaning across the table with a wicked grin. "Obviously, I didn't see everything, because I was trying to get rid of Matthew McGrabby-Hands, who thought it was okay to paw me in the middle of the dance floor, but—"

"Oh, my Godzilla. It was so romantic," Summer says. She leans forward, stealing the gossip spotlight from Emily. "So Shane was, like, watching the door, and waiting for her to show up and all, and the poor kid practically had a heart attack when she finally walked in, he was so freaking nervous."

"Anyway, so he chickens out," Emily says, "but luckily, Pete and Rachel got the D.J. to play your sister's song." She leans back against Pete's chest, and Summer jumps back in to pick up the story.

"Shane asks her to dance, and she says yes, but when the song ends, she rushes over to gush about Adam's singing, and Shane can't figure out how to tell her he wrote it."

"After all those weeks of work," Pete says, "she completely blew him off."

I roll my eyes. "Well, if she thought Adam wrote the song, how was she supposed to know it was for her?"

"It was kinda obvious," Pete says.

"How obvious? Did it mention her by name?"

"No, but 'the girl with the long golden hair' could only be your sister."

"Right. Because there are no other blondes with long hair in the entire school." Shane totally flubbed his chance again. I swear, I have to write a script for that boy. "So she didn't catch on that the song was about her. So what? The important thing is they got together right?"

"Except that's when she ditched him," Emily says.

I shake my head. If she ditched Shane, why was Jarod so sure they'd gotten together?

Summer shrugs. "Kendra asked him to dance and Alaina said they should."

"So Shane and Laina danced one time. And he didn't tell her that the song was for her, because he expected her to read his mind or something. And then Laina stepped aside for the Witch?" I shake my head. That's how Kendra operates. She pushes past Laina every time a boy shows interest in my sister. She even managed to worm her way into a relationship with Jarod back in junior high, by convincing him that he could make Laina jealous if he pretended to date her best friend. They dated for two years before Jarod realized it wasn't going to get him any closer to Laina. But Kendra's managed to twist and manipulate every potential relationship Laina's had ever since. "Shane should've tried again, if he really wanted her. He gave up too soon."

Emily leans across the table. Her eyes widen into her you're-totally-not-gonna-believe-this look and she takes a deep breath. "He tried. But as soon as that second song was over, Laina ran off with Jarod."

I swallow hard and pick at the breading on my corndog. This doesn't sound anything like the story Jarod told me.

Pete smirks. "They were gone for two full hours."

I bite the inside of my cheek and finish dismantling the corn dog. I know exactly what Pete's thinking, and he's got a point. It sure doesn't sound very innocent.

The bell rings, and my friends jump up. "We need to hang out after school," Summer calls over her shoulder.

I shake my head and dump my full tray into the trash can before hurrying after her. "Sorry, we're going over the big ballroom scene tonight. Extra-long rehearsal, right after school. But can you give me a ride to the theater?"

Since Dave and I obviously still aren't speaking, and I'm not ready to face Jarod, I can't rely on them for transportation.

I need to figure out what really happened Saturday night.

The stage lights sparkle against the elaborate palace ballroom sets. Mrs. Mason gives the signal to begin, and I become Arika, the super-sexy, but tragically misunderstood stepsister, who desperately dreams of catching Prince Charming's attention and leaving her bleak existence behind.

When the Page announces my arrival, I float down the stairs at the back of the stage, out into the palace with my sister and mother at my sides. Prince Charming bows and kisses our hands before turning to receive the next arrivals. He's supposed to be bored and politely unresponsive as he greets his guests until Cinderella arrives, but I can't help noticing the way he watches me in a decidedly un-bored way.

"Let's pause for a moment," Mrs. Mason says. She

jumps up onto the stage and crosses to the assembly of lords and ladies filing past the Prince. "I like this, Jarod. It's exactly what I mean when I say you should embrace your character." She smiles at us all, and then returns her focus to Jarod. "But I'd like to see you really play up the twist. Let's make it obvious, so the audience won't miss it."

Mrs. Mason turns to Kathy and Rebekah, the girls playing my mom and sister. "Rebekah, you were standing directly between Andi and the audience on the left side of the theater, so at least half of our audience wouldn't have caught on to the building tension. I need you to stand here instead." She moves Rebekah upstage, away from the audience, and brings me forward, half a step closer to Jarod. "There. Much better."

Jarod frowns and runs his fingers through his hair. He clears his throat and raises his hand. "Um, what do you want me to do?"

Mrs. Mason smiles. "I like your interpretation, but give us a little bit more. Of course Prince Charming might be attracted to other girls before he meets Cinderella. And I love that you've chosen her wicked stepsister to tempt him. But remember, live theater isn't about subtleties. The audience may not catch the twist unless you really play it up."

She grabs my hand and pulls me forward. "Jarod, when you bow and kiss the stepsisters' hands, let's have you address stepsister number two first, and then when she steps out of the way, you turn your full attention to Andi. That look you gave her was absolutely perfect, but remember, only the first row or two will see your face. You have to mirror the look in your body language. Take a step toward her. Hold her hand a little too long. Compliment her. Make it obvious when you watch her walk away. By the time you turn to the next person in the receiving line, I want the audience to wonder if Cinderella will really get the Prince in the end."

"We're working with a classic everyone loves," Curtis

says, "but if we want our performance to stand out, we have to give them a reason to really root for ol' Cindy."

Jarod nods and steps closer to me. He reaches for my hand, but I step back.

"Won't that make Prince Charming, look like a jerk?" I ask. "If he's flirting with me and then dumps me for my sister? The Prince shouldn't be a player."

"You've got a valid point," says Mrs. Mason. "He should be a real person." She studies the crowd of assorted extras. "Let's see … you, you, and you." She pulls three other girls out of the crowd. "Jarod, most of the girls who parade past you in this scene will be nothing more than boring faces in the crowd. But I'd like you to take a half-second to really look at these girls before you dismiss them." She waits until everyone nods, before she continues. "And when Andi comes in, I want the whole auditorium charged with sexual tension. You are really attracted to her. She's beautiful. But it's more than that. You feel a connection to her that defies propriety and protocol. And poor Cinderella may have missed her chance with you, because you're totally smitten."

I giggle. Who says "smitten" anymore?

"That should be easy." Jarod squeezes my hand, and my heart skips a few beats before racing to catch up.

"Good. Let's try it." Mrs. Mason glances over her shoulder. "Curtis? Do we need to change entrances?"

"Not much," he says. "Andi, I'd like you to come in the way we've rehearsed. But Jarod, once Andi catches your attention, you'll bow and smile without even acknowledging the other girls. Keep your eyes focused on Andi. She might be the one you've been waiting for all along."

Jarod nods. "She is."

Curtis smiles and turns his attention to the rest of the cast. "I want to go straight from introductions into the dance. We'll cut the dialogue between the King and Queen. Prince Charming will pass from girl to girl, dancing with everyone for a few seconds, but save stepsister number one for last."

Jarod smiles, and Gretchen and Rebekah take a step toward each other, as if they're already mentally shuffling their onstage positions.

Curtis turns his attention to me. "Andi, when you leave the receiving line, you'll walk to this point, where Chase will approach you, for the dance." He smiles and pulls me into a waltz position. He dances me around the perimeter of the stage, watching Jarod the whole time. "When you reach this point, at the bottom of the stairs, you'll switch partners, but I'd like you to dance with Alex instead of Nathaniel."

I wiggle my toes happily. No Nathaniel means my feet are now safe from trampling.

Nathaniel starts to object, but his protest fades away under Mrs. Mason's glare.

"You're too tall, Nathaniel," she says. "Jarod can't see Andi through you."

Curtis nods and looks from me to Jarod and back again. "Jarod, your eyes should meet Andi's at least once every third time you turn, no matter who you're dancing with. Let your gaze linger as long as possible. Allow the sexual tension build, so the audience is on the edge of their seats by the time you meet in the center of the dance floor."

He stops abruptly and hands me off into Prince Charming's waiting arms. I swallow hard and nod, focusing my gaze on Jarod's shoulder, so I won't have to meet his eyes. Still, I can feel his gaze drilling into me while he pulls me into a tight embrace, and I can't help blushing.

"Good," Curtis says. "Exactly like that, Jarod. And this shy, slightly insecure vibe I'm getting from you is very believable, Andi. But maybe dial it back a bit. Remember, your character isn't afraid to go after what she wants. Let Cinderella be the insecure one."

He steps back and studies us. "Let's draw out the dance to a full minute. Long enough to make the audience believe that you really might run off with Andi." He runs across the stage, grabs Cara's hand, and pulls her to the top of the stairs. "But when ol' Cindy comes in, she totally blows her stepsister out of the water."

Curtis walks down the stairs, imitating the hesitant way he's asked Cara to enter the ballroom scene. He stops in front of Jarod, bats his eyelashes a few times, and curtsies. When the laughter dies down, Curtis turns to me and grins. "When Jarod abandons you to dance with Cara, that's when you'll rejoin Rebekah for your duet. I want you to imagine how it would feel to be second best. You really believed he wanted you."

I bite my lip and nod, stealing a quick look at Jarod. "What if the Prince really does choose the stepsister?"

Jarod blushes and ducks his head.

"We can't rewrite the whole play," Mrs. Mason says. "This is enough." She claps her hands and shoos us all off the stage. "I'll work on the dialogue tonight. For now, let's ad-lib. I'd like to get the choreography set before we leave."

Chapter Twenty-Five

Emily shoves her books into her backpack and slams her locker. "You're no fun anymore. You finally have a day when you're not stuck in rehearsals for that play, and you're still ditching us."

I wince and rub my forehead with my fingertips. "Sorry, Em. If I didn't have this headache, you know I'd go out with you." I give her a shaky smile and sigh. "You think this is how I want to spend my one free afternoon?"

Summer rolls her eyes and jingles her car keys. "Don't bother, Em. She's got a headache. It's too bad there's no little miracle pill to cure something like that."

Emily smirks at me and follows Summer out to the parking lot. "Someone should totally invent some kind of medicine to cure headaches. They'd be freaking rich."

"Ha ha. Very funny." I laugh weakly as I trail behind my friends. "I took some Tylenol before fifth period. It didn't help. Can you just take me home so I can go to bed? I promise

I'll call you if the headache goes away."

I crawl into the back seat of Summer's car and close my eyes, tuning out Emily's play-by-play of her conversation with Pete last night. A headache is the most cliché excuse in the world, but I'm desperate. It's been nearly a week since prom, and today might be my only chance to find out what really happened.

Laina's studying with Kendra, and Mom goes grocery shopping on Thursdays. I need to sneak into Laina's room and steal her diary before anyone gets home.

I drag myself out of Summer's car and slowly up the steps to the front door. But as soon as Summer drives away, I sprint into the house and down the hall to Mom and Dad's bedroom. I force myself to slow down and carefully search through Mom's jewelry box for the spare key to Laina's room, leaving everything else in the box, exactly as I found it.

Laina almost always keeps her current diary with her, so there's not much chance that I'll find that one, but I glance at her old hiding space under her pillow anyway.

Nope.

I reach under Laina's bed for the wooden box where she keeps her old diaries. A large combination lock dangles from the latch, but this is the easy part. Last year, I forgot the combination to the padlock on my gym locker, and a quick internet search showed me how easy they are to crack. It takes less than a minute to access Laina's stash of secrets.

I grab the notebook on top of the stack and flip to the date label Laina has written on the inside front cover. Thursday, March twenty-fourth through Monday, April eleventh.

I have the entire prom story in my hands.

After locking the box and sliding it back under the bed, I open Laina's door a crack to make sure the coast is clear. Mom is in the kitchen, putting groceries away, close enough to hear me if I'm not careful. I tuck the diary into the waistband of my jeans and pull my shirt down over it, and then slowly open the door until there's enough room to slip out. I hold the knob as I close the door, so it won't make a sound, then quickly re-lock it and slip the key into my pocket. I'll put it back in Mom's jewelry box after I return the diary.

I tiptoe down the hall to my bedroom and sink into my bed. Closing my eyes, I concentrate on taking deep breaths to steady my breathing and return my heart rate to normal before pulling out the book.

I turn to the entry labeled Sunday, April 10, 1:07am. Minutes after she got home from the prom.

Dear Diary,

Andi was right. Prom sucks. I should have gone bowling with her and Nick instead. I still would've been a third wheel, but at least I might have had some fun.

Maybe I'm imagining things, but when Nick came to pick up Andi before I left, I think he was kind of flirting with me a little bit. Even though I'm sure he was only doing it to get a reaction out of Andi, it was kind of cool to be the center of attention for once, instead of constantly living in my baby sister's shadow. For a few minutes, I could pretend that I'm almost as pretty as she is.

Is she freaking serious? I emit a loud snort of laughter, but I quickly clap my hand over my mouth to stifle the sound, so Mom won't come in to see what's going on.

I re-read the page, but it still says the same thing. Laina thinks she has to compete with me for attention. How can she not realize how much every guy in the world totally worships her?

I skim through the rest of her description of Nick's flirting, and her pre-prom dinner, where Kendra did her best to undo everything Nick had accomplished.

Kendra kept pinching the tiny roll of flab on her waistline and worrying that her dress made her look as huge as me. She almost decided we'd have to skip prom.

I would kill to get the kind of attention Kendra does. When we walked into the dance, I overheard a couple of guys from my chemistry class talking. I don't know if they were being loud on purpose, or if they thought the music would drown them out, but I didn't think they were talking about me, so I wasn't paying much attention until Kendra nudged me. I missed the first part of what they were saying, but I heard enough.

"Check it out. Beauty and the Beast."

"I don't get it. Why are they even friends?"

"Ignore them," Kendra said, quickly pulling me across the room and out of earshot. "You shouldn't worry about the way guys compare us."

But that's easier said than done.

"If they can't see past your lopsided figure to who you are inside, you don't need them," Kendra said.

And she's totally right. I shouldn't pay attention. But it would be easier to ignore the comments if she didn't always point them out in the first place.

I'll never understand how someone as gorgeous and perfect as Laina can believe Kendra's lies. It's beyond obvious that she didn't want Laina to pay attention because she didn't want her to realize exactly who the guys were calling a beast.

But then it didn't matter, because Shane asked me to dance. He even said I looked beautiful. I know it doesn't count, because guys are required to tell girls they look pretty at times like this, but he said it to me and not to Rachel who, by the way, looked absolutely amazing in that emerald green dress Kendra wouldn't let me buy.

She gushes for three whole pages about Shane's song. Of course, she thought Adam wrote it, and Shane didn't say anything to set her straight. He only told her he'd talk to Adam and Pete to get a copy for her, since she liked it so much.

Because he's an idiot, obviously.

It takes me over an hour to finish reading the prom story, which fills up more than half the notebook and includes every single detail, including the name of her waiter at dinner and the number of fake torches lining the walls in the gym. It's no wonder Laina spent all weekend locked in her room.

Kendra did everything she could to get between Shane and Laina. She managed to convince my sister that he was only pretending to be interested, because he thought Laina would sleep with him after prom. The way he held her a little too close while they were dancing, combined with the stupid things he said when we visited him at Burger Barn, made it too easy for Laina to believe Kendra's version of the story.

And when Kendra called Laina a slut for dancing with Shane a second time, after Kendra "warned" her about his "true intentions," Laina gave up and left the prom in tears. Jarod, her faithful knight in shining armor, followed her.

And nothing happened.

She cried on his shoulder, which explains the makeup smudges on his jacket. But she wouldn't tell him what she was crying about, because Kendra and Shane are the two topics she avoids discussing with Jarod. And they held hands and walked around the parking lot a few times until she was smiling again.

When we finally went back into the gym, Jarod started singing along with that old Bruno Mars song, "Just the Way You Are." He told me it's my theme song, because I'm perfect. Only Jarod would be so cheesy and so totally clueless that he wouldn't even realize he was singing a love song at me.

And obviously, Laina and I are both idiots. Neither of us wants to admit how much Jarod is still in love with her. And maybe I'm as bad as Kendra. I haven't exactly been selflessly helping her to find true love all this time.

Then the last song started playing, and Shane and Jarod both asked me to dance. For a minute, it looked like they might start fighting right in the middle of the dance floor. (Whatever they're fighting about keeps threatening to boil over with me right in the middle of it all.) But once again, Jarod proved that he's the best friend I could ever have. He obviously knew how much I wanted to dance with Shane. How much I wanted a second chance at the fairy tale. Jarod hugged me and left without saying a word. I guess, after the crappy night I had, he wanted me to have something good to remember about prom.

Or maybe he saw that she'd made her choice. What was it he said when he came over? "You should've seen the way her eyes lit up when he asked her to dance." She didn't have to tell him that she wanted Shane. He could see it in her eyes. And he's so freaking in love with her that he just walked away, because that's what she wanted.

I should've been happy, but I couldn't convince myself that any of it was real. I know what he said to Kendra. I know he's not really interested in the real me. Shane is like Anthony. Maybe all boys are.

Except Jarod.

He's my personal White Knight, racing to the rescue whenever I need saving. And sometimes I think it's not really fair to him. He shouldn't have to always put himself last while he tends to my drama. But I still shudder when I think about what would've happened if Jarod hadn't been there last year. There's no way I could've survived the thing with Anthony on my own.

I almost wish I'd ended the night dancing with Jarod instead of Shane. Because even though we're only friends, I know Jarod and I are a team forever. And after the last dance was over—

Laina's diary entry cuts off mid-sentence and I stifle a frustrated scream. She must've run out of room in this notebook and simply grabbed a new one to finish the thought. And there's no way I'm getting my hands on her current diary.

Not until she fills it up.

Back when I used to sneak her diaries all the time, she would never have left a thought unfinished. Sometimes, she'd even glue in extra pages to accommodate the end of a journal entry. But that was back when she was still using expensive, leather-bound journals and keeping them neatly shelved. Before she switched to spiral-bound notebooks shoved in a box.

I close the notebook and slip it under my mattress. I may not have the whole story, but these things I know for sure:

1. Laina is still in love with Jarod, whether she admits it to herself or not.
2. Jarod is obviously still in love with Laina.
3. Whatever happened last year with Anthony Matthews, it's still bothering her more than she wants to admit.
4. I'm afraid to think about what happened. Because I have a sneaking suspicion that I know what it was.

I consider going back to Laina's room to find the answer in her old diaries, but I can hear Mom watching TV in the family room, and she would totally see me if I tried to get in there now. Besides, there must be a zillion books from last year, and without a more specific time frame, I'll never be able to find the one with the Anthony Matthews incident.

But Jarod was there. He can tell me what happened.

Chapter Twenty-Six

I corner Jarod at his locker before school.

"Can we talk?" I ask. "Privately?"

His eyes light up, and he slides his arm around my waist. "Sure. Why don't I give you a ride to rehearsal tonight? We can talk then."

I pull away and shake my head, trying not to notice the butterflies in my stomach that started fluttering like crazy the second he looked at me. I wish I could ignore the way his eyes flit up and down the hall to make sure no one is paying attention to us, but I can't. "No, it has to be now. But only talking. No touching."

I lead him to the south stairs and take a deep breath to calm my nerves. Other than rehearsals, I've been avoiding him since prom night. Not that it's done any good. Dave still won't talk to me.

I think about the way Jarod kissed me in the kitchen, the way his touch sent tingles up and down my spine, even though I knew it was wrong, and I have to cross my arms to avoid reaching for him now. And when he looks at me with those emerald eyes and runs his fingers through his hair, I know he's feeling the same way.

Maybe a private chat with Jarod wasn't such a great idea after all.

I shake my head. Our personal issues can wait. "What happened with Anthony Matthews?"

Jarod frowns. "Um, nothing? I don't really hang out with losers." He reaches for me, and his fingertips graze my shoulder before he remembers my no touching rule and pulls away again.

"Last year." I take a deep breath and exhale slowly. "What happened with Anthony and Laina?"

The color drains form Jarod's face and his jaw clenches. "Why? What did you hear?"

I bite my cheek. "Well, I kind of stole Laina's diary to find out what really happened on prom night." I shrug. "You know how Laina is. She writes down every detail about every single, little thing that ever happens to her." I study his face, looking for clues. "But she keeps making vague references to something that happened last year with Anthony, and she never elaborates."

"Maybe it's so unimportant that it's not worth writing down the details?" Jarod looks so hopeful that I wish I could believe him.

"She spent half a page describing the flavor of the pasta she ate for dinner before prom. Laina doesn't do vague. Not in her diaries. If it's important enough to mention, she's going to record every detail." I think about her meticulous description of the waiter who smiled at her during dinner and the long, boring pages where she listed every element of the prom décor. "Why would she bring up the thing that happened with Anthony and then skip the specifics?"

"Maybe she wrote about it all when it happened, and

so she doesn't need to think about it anymore?"

I shake my head. "No. She's actively trying to not remember." I take a deep breath, carefully watching Jarod's reactions. His eyes narrow and he clenches his hands into tight fists, but he doesn't say a word.

"I was only going to read the entry from prom night," I say, "but she kept mentioning the thing that happened with Anthony. I thought I might find some clues if I read more. So I read it all. The diary only covers a couple of weeks, but Laina refers to that incident with Anthony on almost every page."

I bite my lip and study Jarod's eyes. He doesn't say anything.

"The thing is, she thinks about Anthony whenever she writes about any guy who pays attention to her. And it's like it makes her nervous. Or ashamed. Maybe even terrified." I exhale slowly, letting all of the pent-up emotion spill out of me along with the tears I can't hold back anymore. "Tell me I'm wrong."

Jarod slams his fist into the door. "I'm so stupid," he mutters. "I should've known she wasn't okay, but I didn't want to believe it was so bad. I should've forced her to talk to someone, to do something. I should've killed Matthews."

I swallow hard and try to force the words out. "Did he …?" I can't bring myself to ask. I don't want him to confirm my fears. I close my eyes and try to block the image of Laina, torn and broken, from my mind.

It's no wonder she's so skittish.

"Of course not," Jarod growls. "Do you think I'd let Matthews live if he'd raped her?"

I heave a sigh of relief and collapse onto the bottom step. I should've known I was reading too much into everything. She would have told me if something like that happened. She wouldn't have tried to suffer through it in silence. I always give Laina a hard time about her overactive imagination, but I've obviously seen too many TV dramas for my own good.

"But he tried," Jarod whispers.

My blood chills as I look up to see the tortured look in his eyes. I reach for his hand and pull him down to sit on the steps with me.

There are no words.

The bell rings, and we ignore it. We sit silently on the steps as kids file past us on their way to class, waiting until the stairs are empty again before resuming our conversation. I lean against Jarod's shoulder and squeeze his hand, and for once there's no sexual tension charging the air between us.

There's nothing but Laina.

Once we're alone again, Jarod clears his throat. "Remember the State Marching Band competition last year?"

I bury my face in my hands. I should have known that losing the competition wasn't enough to make Laina lose herself. I should have forced her to talk to me sooner. "What happened?"

A tear slips down Jarod's cheek. "It's my fault. I should have been there."

"What?"

"Matthews was whining about Savannah dumping him, and Laina felt sorry for him. I should never have let them out of my sight." He stares blankly at the wall, cringing as if he's watching the whole thing again. "When they didn't show up for the pre-show warm-ups, I went looking for Laina. I heard her screaming."

I squeeze his hand and wait for him to continue, even though I want to cover my ears. Pretending it didn't happen won't help Laina.

Anthony had trapped her in an empty stairwell behind the marching arena, and by the time Jarod found them, Laina was hiding in a corner, using a large trash can as a shield. Her uniform top was torn open and the thin t-shirt she wore underneath was ripped. Jarod had knocked Anthony out with a few good punches, and he got Laina away from the creep, but she wouldn't let him report it to Mrs. Harmony.

Laina was afraid that, if anyone found out about the attack, they'd think she did something to encourage him. She was afraid people might talk about her or say it was her fault. Or worse. And she was probably right.

People are idiots.

Jarod leans his head on my shoulder and hugs me just a little too tight. "He didn't rape her. And I thought, since I stopped him before he could actually do anything, that she was okay. I thought we could forget about it. Like it never happened." He runs his fingers through his hair, exhaling forcefully. "She hasn't mentioned it since. Never even hinted that it was still bothering her." He stands up and turns away from me. "I screwed up."

"You didn't know," I say, scrambling to my feet. "You couldn't have known what she was feeling. No one did." I look at the chipped paint on the wall and suppress a shudder. Laina was attacked in an empty stairwell like this. In a crowded stadium, with thousands of people, Jarod was the only one who heard her call for help. If he hadn't gone looking for her …

I shiver. "But we know now. You need to report Anthony to Mrs. Gardner. I know it was last year, but this is serious. It can't be too late for someone to do something." I kick at a loose tile on the floor. "Or go to the police. I know he didn't actually … I mean, you stopped it, right? But isn't what he did still illegal?"

"Could they even do anything without proof?"

"Well, they have to investigate, right? They can't just let him get away with it."

"I don't think we can go to the police if Laina refuses to talk about it." Jarod slumps against the wall. "I should have said something last year. I didn't want to make it worse by forcing her to face it when she wanted to forget. And I wouldn't even know who to talk to now. We're seniors now, so we can't report him to the junior class counselor, right? And Ms. Cram wouldn't be able to help, would she? Since it happened when we were juniors, not seniors?"

"So talk to both counselors. They can work together."

He hits his head against the wall. "If Laina doesn't want anyone to know, shouldn't we respect her wishes?"

"I won't sit back and watch her entire world crumble, if I can do something about it. I don't care if it's not our story to tell."

Jarod kicks the bottom step. "I know. But we need her to speak up for herself. Without Laina, it'll be our word against his, and you weren't even there." He sits on the bottom step and pulls me down beside him. "What if she refuses to talk about it? What if she says we're making it all up? Not only will that slime ball get away with everything, but we'll be causing Laina pain for no reason. There has to be a better way."

I consider going to the counselor on my own, but I don't even know enough of the details to make anyone listen to me. I can't do this without Jarod, and he won't do it without Laina. So we spend the next thirty-five minutes trying to come up with a plan to help Laina take control over her life.

And we've got nothing.

When the bell rings to end second period, Jarod stands and brushes the dirt off his pants. "I have to get to class," he says. "I can't miss this test."

I nod and stand up as well. He reaches for the door to the stairs, but I grab his arm to stop him. "Jarod? One last thing." I don't want to say it, but he has a right to know. "Laina didn't choose Shane on Saturday night. She's afraid to choose anyone. She won't let anyone in because of this." I look away. "So if we can help her get past the thing with Anthony, I guess you still have a chance."

He hugs me and his lips brush my forehead. "Thanks,"

he says. And then he runs off to class.

I watch him go and wonder if I did the right thing. Dave doesn't want me anymore, and I may have destroyed every chance I have with Jarod, but I meant what I said on prom night.

I'm done with secrets and manipulation.

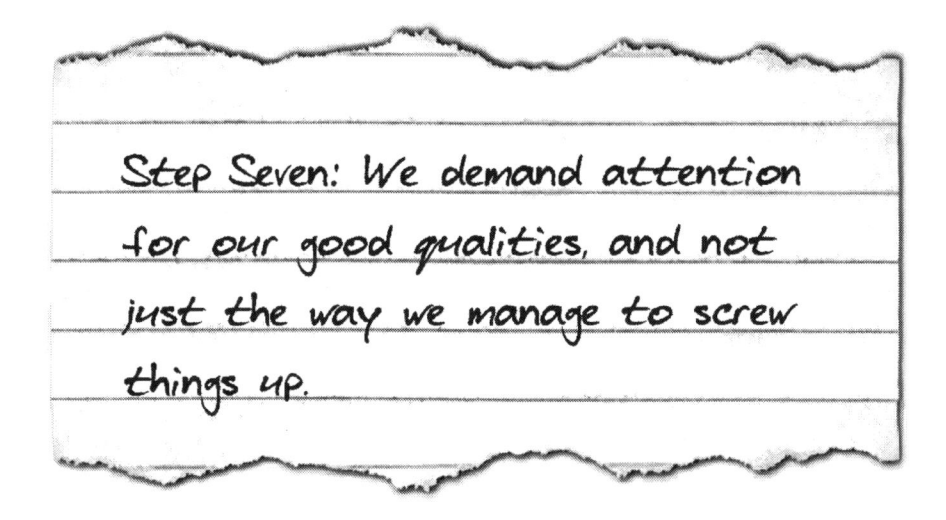

Step Seven: We demand attention for our good qualities, and not just the way we manage to screw things up.

Chapter Twenty-Seven

Mom's waiting in the living room when I get home from school. She waves a folded piece of paper at me and frowns. "We need to talk."

Unfortunately, I recognize that frown. I see the Andi-isn't-living-up-to-her-full-potential frown way more than I want to admit. I take a deep breath and sit on the couch, waiting for the lecture I know is coming.

Mom waves the paper at me again. "I got your midterm progress report. I thought you said you were going to bring up your biology grade." She hands the paper to me, and her frown deepens. "Why are you failing?"

I groan and open the page. I still have As and Bs in all of my other classes, but my biology grade is even worse.

Fifty-seven percent.

It's not like I'm not trying.

I do my homework. Most of the time.

And I've been trying to pay attention in class. But biology is so boring. And Mr. Keeler has the kind of voice that no amount of caffeine can combat. It takes every ounce of my concentration not to fall asleep in class. I can't help it if his lectures are too mind-numbing to listen to.

"I'm afraid, until you bring your grade up to at least a C, you'll have to forego any and all extracurricular activities." Mom takes the report card back and shakes her head. "That includes acting. You'll need to call Mrs. Mason to let her know that you will no longer be participating in *Cinderella*."

"What? No!" I grab Mom's hands and give her my best sad puppy dog eyes. "I can't quit now. Opening night is next Friday. And I've worked so hard. Please don't take this away from me."

Mom sighs. "I'm sorry, sweetheart. I know how much this play means to you. I'm so proud of you, and I don't want to be the bad guy here, but your academics have to come first. No arguments."

I bite my lip and blink back tears. Crying only works on Dad. Never with Mom. Especially not when she's already made up her mind. My only hope is to calmly give her another option. One that will let her feel like she's doing the motherly discipline thing right while still giving me what I want.

"What if I get a tutor?" I ask. "I promise I'll work really hard to pull up my grade, but please let me stick with *Cinderella*."

Mom shakes her head. "Sorry, sweetie, but until I see actual proof of improvement, I can't agree. Acting may be a fun, creative outlet, but your biology grade will have a real impact on your future. Failing a class won't look good on your transcripts, and colleges pay attention to things like this, even if you don't plan on majoring in science." She holds out the phone. "Call Mrs. Mason. Let her know you won't be at tonight's practice. She'll need time to get your understudy ready for the part."

I take the phone and hold it in my lap. "I have a quiz on

Wednesday. Can I have until then to prove myself? I'll call a tutor right now. Two days won't make much of a difference, will it?" I bite my lip and clasp my hands together, pleading for her to understand. "Can I please keep going to rehearsals until then? I promise, I'll let Mrs. Mason know that I'm on academic probation, so she can start working with the understudy. And if I don't get at least a B on Wednesday's quiz, I'll quit. No questions asked. And you can ground me for the rest of the year. Or make me clean out the attic. Whatever. Just give me one more chance. I can do this, I swear."

Mom frowns, but I can tell she's weakening.

"Please, Mommy, I love you." I blink my sad, puppy-dog eyes at her. "You're the best Mommy in the whole expanding universe." I stick out my bottom lip in a totally exaggerated pout. "And I will be so sad if you say no."

I snuggle up to her, like I did when I was five. "And I'll make dinner for you, while you relax in a bubble bath, if you say yes."

Mom laughs and throws her hands in the air. "All right. Fine. You win. But I'll take a rain check on dinner and that bubble bath. I already have dinner in the crock pot for tonight, and you have to study. Call a tutor right now, because you need to put in at least forty-five minutes of true study time before dinner, or you will not be going to rehearsal tonight."

"Thank you, thank you, thank you!" I tackle her with a massive hug. Then, I grab the phone and punch in Dave's number. He aced advanced biology last year, so I know he can help. I only hope he'll talk to me.

It takes less than I expected to convince Dave. After only five minutes' worth of begging, and the promise of Mom's homemade beef stew for dinner, he agrees to come over before rehearsal. And he's standing on the doorstep, books in hand, almost before I can hang up the phone.

"But if I'm going to tutor you," he says, "I expect your full attention. No Andi mind games or manipulation. I'm not wasting my time if you're not serious."

"Yeah, of course. I need to pass this class. I'll do whatever you say. Whatever it takes. I'm yours." I cringe as soon as the words are out of my mouth. I expect him to throw out some cheesy line about how he could think of a lot of things for me to do or something stupid like that, but he just smiles and settles in at the kitchen table with his books.

"So if parent A has blue eyes and parent B has brown eyes, what is the probability that their child will be born with blue eyes?"

I blink. "Um … fifty percent, I guess?" We've been studying for an hour, but I still have no idea what he's talking about.

"Why do you guess that answer?"

I stare at the chart in the text book, with the list of dominant and recessive traits. "I don't know. I don't understand any of this." I toss my pencil onto the table, and it rolls over the edge and bounces on its eraser before settling next to Dave's scuffed cowboy boot. "I don't see how the information you gave me is enough to figure it out."

Dave grins and retrieves my pencil. "Correct." He turns the page in the textbook and points to a table printed on the bottom corner of the paper. "Because of recessive and dominant genes, you need at least two generations' data, or an analysis of the parent DNA, to begin to accurately predict something like eye color." He looks into my eyes and smiles. "Why is that?"

I know I should be getting this by now, and Dave is definitely more interesting than Mr. Keeler. But I can't focus. I need to stop getting distracted by Dave's dimples.

"Okay, let's go back to the basics." Dave smiles again and taps my page of scribbled notes. "How many genes for a specific trait does each person have?"

"Two?"

He nods. "Correct. A baby gets one gene from his father and one from his mother. So if his father and his mother both give him a brown-eyes gene, then his eyes will be?"

"Brown."

"See? It's simple. So, if both parents give the baby a blue-eyes gene, what color will his eyes be?"

"Blue." I shrug. "It's easy when there's no mixing involved. But all of the dominant, recessive, who-has-what-gene stuff gets confusing."

"Nah, it's easy. You're only making it harder than it has to be." Dave glances at his watch, and I bite my lip. Is he going to declare me a lost cause? He takes a deep breath and taps my forehead. "Okay, you can do this. I want you to take your time and really think about it. What happens if the dad gives the baby a blue-eyes gene and the mom gives him a brown-eyes gene? What color will the baby's eyes be?"

"Brown?"

"Why?"

"Because brown is dominant and blue is recessive?"

"Yes!" Dave hugs me and I breathe in the musky scent of his aftershave. The combination of old leather and some kind of spice makes my head swim, and I hold onto him a little bit longer than I probably should.

He pulls back, and the way he looks at me makes the butterflies in my stomach kick into high gear. I suddenly feel all light-headed and tingly, and I lean forward, silently giving him permission to kiss me. But before our lips meet, he stands up and slams the textbook shut.

"See? This is the easy stuff. It's all repetition of the same thing. You'll be fine for your quiz, as long as you take the time to really think through your answers." He glances at his watch again. "We'd better get going, or we'll be late for rehearsal." He grabs his keys and stacks the books on the edge of the table. "I'll leave these here for you, in case you want to study some more after rehearsal tonight."

I stand and grab my coat. "Yeah, I'll go tell Mom we're leaving."

Chapter Twenty-Eight

I get one hundred percent on my biology quiz, but Mom says I have to keep up my tutoring sessions with Dave if I want to continue with *Cinderella*. I don't mind, actually. Biology isn't so hard when Dave explains it. He gets so excited that it's even kind of fun.

Even better, all of the weird awkwardness that cropped up around the prom is gone, and we're back to our easy friendship. It's a good thing I didn't kiss him when I wanted to last week. I would have screwed everything up again.

Dave always insisted that it's impossible for guys and girls to be just friends, but "just friends" is the only relationship that works for us. When we started spending too much time with each other, and everyone thought we were together, when I thought I was falling in love with him, that's when everything got weird and fell apart.

"Good job on that quiz," Dave says, pulling out a notebook and pen. He grabs an Oreo from my plate and dunks it in my milk. "Now, let's keep it up for the actual unit test, okay?"

"Hey! Get your own." I pull my cookies and milk out of his reach.

He pops the Oreo into his mouth, and then he grins, showing off his gross, cookie coated teeth.

"Ewww. That's disgusting, and these are mine. Don't you have any sense of boundaries?"

He leans across the table and snatches another Oreo off of my plate. "It's not my fault you're a bad hostess. You could offer me some cookies and milk, and then I wouldn't have to take yours."

"I did offer, when you got here, remember? You said you don't like Oreos. So keep your paws off."

He smiles and takes another cookie. "Well, you should have offered me something else. It's rude to eat in front of your empty-handed guests. I'm trying to help you be polite."

I grab the package of Oreos out of the cupboard. Then, I pour another glass of milk for myself and slide the cup he's been sneaking sips from across the table to Dave. "There, now leave my snack alone. You're here to help with my biology, not to binge on junk food."

He laughs again and drains his cup of milk. He reaches for mine next, but I pull it out of the way and shoot him a dirty look.

"Okay, okay," he says. "Man, you're cranky today." He opens my textbook to the chapter about genetics and smiles. "Are we gonna study, or are you planning on playing around all afternoon?"

I punch him in the arm.

"Ouch!" He flips through pages in the textbook as he rubs his arm. "Someone got the aggressive, hot-girl gene. Is that a dominant or recessive trait?"

I laugh. "Well, amazing hotness does run in my family. But the aggressiveness is only a reaction to your super-jerk gene."

"Oh, really?" Dave jumps up and lunges at me. He grabs me around the waist, and when he starts tickling, I shriek and squirm away. I grab the towel that's hanging on the handle of the refrigerator and snap it at him.

"Stay back," I warn. "I know how to use this."

"Oh, I think I can handle it." He advances on me slowly, hands outstretched.

I flick the towel at him furiously, but I'm laughing so hard that my aim is terrible, and I miss him every time.

Dad walks into the kitchen and stands in the middle of the room with his hands on his hips and a giant frown on his face. "I don't see much studying going on in here," he says. "Dave, is this what we're paying you for?"

"No, sir." Dave drops his hands to his sides and returns to his seat at the kitchen table. He consults the study sheet Mr. Keeler gave us. "Who was the father of modern genetics?"

One glance at Dad's giant scowl tells me this isn't the time to point out that Dave is helping me for free, and we aren't actually paying him. I slink back to the table and try to focus on biology.

Dad watches us for a few minutes, and then he stomps out of the room. But I'm totally not surprised when Laina decides half a minute later that the kitchen table is way more comfortable than the huge, overstuffed reading chair in her bedroom for reading her English lit assignment. Even though she always swears she can't concentrate on her homework when there are other people around.

When Dave leaves an hour later, Laina sighs and closes her book. "I didn't know you and Dave were back together."

"We're not 'back together.' We were never together in the first place. And we're not 'together' now. We're friends. Like you and Jarod."

Except, of course, for the whole being secretly in love with each other thing.

She raises one eyebrow at me. "Dad made it sound like

you guys were getting pretty intense in here." She glances at the front door, like she expects to see Dave still standing there, even though he's long gone, and then she turns her attention back to me. "Be careful, okay? You don't want to give a guy the wrong ideas."

I shiver as I look into her hollow, empty eyes. I don't think she's talking about me and Dave anymore.

"What do you mean? What kind of ideas?" Maybe if I keep her talking, I can finally get her to open up about Anthony.

Laina laughs, but the smile doesn't reach her eyes. "How serious are things with you and Dave? What exactly is going on between you?"

I bite my lip and follow Laina's gaze to the front door. I'm in love with Jarod. I've been in love with him since I was eleven years old. And I think he's starting to like me, too. The way he holds me when we're dancing the ballroom scene can't all be an act.

Besides, I missed my chance with Dave. He's made it perfectly clear that he doesn't think about me that way anymore. I can't be in love with him.

"I don't know. It's easier if we're friends."

"Is that what you really want? Because if it is, you have to make sure he knows. You don't want him to think there's more going on."

I shiver and blink back tears. This isn't about me. Laina needs to talk about Anthony, or she'll never get over it. But I can't exactly admit I've been reading her diary. Except, she already knows I read the part about her and Shane. She mentioned Anthony then, too.

"Speaking of friends who are totally in love with you, how are things with Shane these days?"

Laina grabs my biology notes that are strewn across the table and stacks them together in a neat pile on top of my textbook and the study guide Dave left behind. Then, she grabs a paper towel and starts wiping up the stray Oreo crumbs. She acts like she didn't hear and refuses to look at me. I know she heard my question, though, because her hands are shaking like crazy and she keeps twisting the end of her long, blonde curls around her finger.

When she finishes cleaning the kitchen, she turns and flashes her plastic smile at me. "Well, I'm tired. I think I'll go to bed early. See you in the morning."

She bounces out of the room before I can say a word.

I jump up and run after her, but she closes and locks her bedroom door as I catch up. It's totally against the rules for her to lock the door when she's home, because Mom says that "locking yourself away from your own family puts you in a compromising position and allows you to slip into highly inappropriate behavior." I could tell Dad that she locked me out, and he'd make her open the door, but there's no way Laina will open up to me about Anthony or anything else if I bring Mom and Dad into this.

Laina and I haven't had a real conversation since before the prom, and I totally blew the first chance I got.

I stumble down the hall to my bedroom and throw myself across the bed to stare at the ceiling. How can I help her to get past that thing with Anthony if I screw it up every time I try to get her to talk to me?

I close my eyes and try to ignore the answer I don't really want to see.

Jarod was there. And he saved her. Laina might talk to him. Maybe she needs him as much as he wants her.

A large tear rolls across my cheek and into my ear. I flip over and bury my face in my pillow. Laina deserves a boyfriend like Jarod. Someone she can talk to about anything and everything. Someone who will always be there for her. Someone who's so afraid of changing the status quo that he may never work up the nerve to actually kiss her, unless she makes the first move.

Someone who will never invade her personal space, like Anthony did.

Maybe I need to pull myself out of the equation and let Laina have Jarod once and for all.

Maybe I need to admit that I was never a part of the equation in the first place.

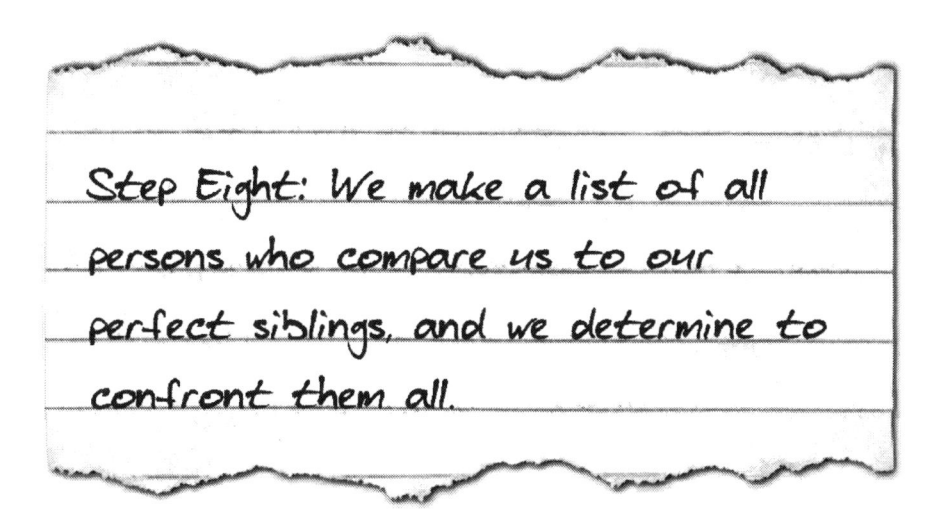

Step Eight: We make a list of all persons who compare us to our perfect siblings, and we determine to confront them all.

Chapter Twenty-Nine

Mr. Keeler stands in front of the classroom, a stack of graded papers in his hands. "Some of you obviously didn't study for this test, and I'm very disappointed in the results." He looks straight at me and frowns.

Crap! This was the first time all year that I felt like I was really prepared for a biology exam. So much for my delusions.

I fill the margins of my notebook with doodles of DNA strands and daisies, breathing slowly and thinking back over the exam questions as I wait for him to hand back the tests. Maybe he's not talking about me.

I was ready.

I know this stuff.

I almost laugh out loud when I imagine Dave shaking his head and accusing me of giving in to my "pessimistic pretty girl gene." But when Mr. Keeler slips my paper, face down, onto my desk, the urge to giggle fades, and I have to swallow hard to keep down the bile rising in my throat.

I take a deep breath and hold it for ten seconds before letting it out slowly.

I let my eyes roam around the room, watching as everyone else looks at their scores. A couple of people look like they want to cry, and a couple of them are obviously thrilled, but most glance at their scores and tuck the papers into their notebooks without any kind of reaction.

I close my eyes and turn my exam over. Then, I take another slow, deep breath and open my left eye just a crack to see.

Nothing.

Not a single question is marked wrong on my paper, but I have a giant, red zero across the page, and a tiny, scrawled note in the top, left corner that says "See me after class."

I spend the next fifty-five minutes searching through my textbook to check my answers, and as far as I can tell, I haven't missed any of them. Why did I get a zero?

Mr. Keeler might hate me, but he knows I would never cheat. Maybe it's a minus zero. As in one hundred percent. Maybe he's impressed with my hard work and initiative in bringing up my grades. He probably wants me to stay after class so he can congratulate me on my hard work and study.

It could happen.

Right?

The hour drags on for a million years, but finally the bell rings and everyone files out of the classroom. I wipe my palms on my jeans, and then I grab my stack of books and make my way to Mr. Keeler's desk at the front of the room.

He glances at me and frowns, and then he opens his grade book and pulls out a stack of papers. He doesn't look up again as he starts entering grades into his book.

I fidget for a minute or two, waiting for him to speak, but he doesn't even act like he knows I'm here. Did he not want to speak with me after all? Maybe he changed his mind. Or maybe he wrote the note on the wrong test paper.

I clear my throat and wait for another thirty seconds, but he still doesn't look up. When the warning bell rings for next period, I give up and turn to leave. Mr. Keeler may have a free period next, but I don't. And I'll never be anything but Laina's little, screw-up sister if I don't start demonstrating that I can be as good as she is. I can't afford to let my grades slip in my other classes, too.

I'm reaching for the doorknob when Mr. Keeler finally speaks. "I'm still waiting, Ms. Andersen."

I turn to look at him. His steel-grey eyes bore straight through me, and the harsh scowl on his face tells me that he isn't planning to compliment my study habits. I swallow hard and force a smile.

"Waiting? For what?"

He stands and walks around his desk, closing the space between us. He towers over me, so I have to look up to see his face. I have an overwhelming urge to apologize and throw myself at his feet to beg for mercy.

But I haven't done anything wrong. So I take a deep breath and meet his cold stare with one of my own.

Mr. Keeler breaks before I do. He huffs and crosses his arms. "I don't tolerate cheating in my class, Ms. Andersen. But if you tell me how you managed to get a copy of my answer key, I might go easy on you."

"What?" I feel like I've been punched in the gut. I mean, I'm not stupid. A big, fat zero on my test paper when I didn't miss a single question, and a cryptic note from the teacher saying that he wanted to see me after class. It's a total teacher cliché for cheaters. But still, I'd hoped I was reading the clues wrong.

Mr. Keeler glares at me. "I let it slide on the quiz, because it was only ten points, and I'd hoped that the sister of Alaina Andersen would have the integrity to feel some remorse, and the moral courage to own up to her crime. But this exam counts for one-fifth of your total semester grade, and I cannot tolerate such willful disregard of the school's honor code, no matter who your sister is."

"I didn't cheat. I studied!"

"Ms. Andersen, in my twenty-three years of teaching, I have never had a student get every single question correct on one of my exams, including both bonus questions. Even your sister only got a ninety-nine percent on the genetics exam, and her grade average was the highest I've ever seen. Yet, you want me to believe that you, a student who has been consistently failing my class all year long, managed to pull off a perfect score with a single late-night study session?"

"No."

He smirks, and I can tell he thinks he's bullied me into a confession, but I worked too hard for this to allow him to snatch it all away. I topped Laina's high score. I'm smart enough to deal with a judgmental, arrogant teacher.

"No. It wasn't one study session." I smirk right back at him. "I expect you to believe that this student, who has been failing your class all year long, finally got a tutor who could explain biology without totally putting her to sleep in the process." I clutch my books to my chest, resisting the urge to hurl them at his head. "I wouldn't be so proud of the streak of bad grades spewing out of your class. If even my sister couldn't manage to stay awake in your class long enough to ace a single one of your tests, then maybe you're the problem."

I spin on my heel and stalk out of the room, leaving a spluttering, red-faced Mr. Keeler gaping after me. I know my little outburst probably didn't earn me the student-of-the-year award, but what's the worst he can do? Call my parents? They'll just tell him I've been studying with Dave every night.

I'm not surprised when the call interrupts my English literature class, telling me to report to Ms. Detweiler's office immediately. I totally expected Mr. Keeler to go running to the principal when he realized he couldn't bully me on his own. But I am a little bit surprised to see that my mom is already there when I arrive.

Mr. Keeler, Mom, and Ms. Detweiler sit shoulder-to-shoulder in a row of chairs on one side of the room, and Ms. Detweiler instructs me to have a seat in the empty chair facing them, next to Mrs. Gardner.

I feel like an inmate on death row, facing down the firing squad.

"Andi, dear, we're concerned," Mrs. Gardner says. "Mr. Keeler tells us there was an incident today in class, and we'd like to get to the bottom of it, so that this kind of emotional outburst can be avoided in the future."

I should totally get a million karma points for managing to control the "emotional outburst" I want to unleash right now. I take a deep breath and count to ten before I respond, and when I speak, I make sure to keep my voice calm and even, without even a hint of the anger I feel.

Well, maybe a hint.

"Did he tell you that he accused me of cheating, all because I managed to pass his stupid exam? You'd think a teacher would be grateful that his students are trying to learn, instead of getting all judgy when they work their butts off studying."

Mrs. Gardner sighs. "Andi, dear, you must admit that your story seems a little far-fetched. Do you truly expect us to believe that, when you haven't managed to pass a single biology exam all year long, suddenly you are the first student to honestly earn a perfect score on Mr. Keeler's genetics exam?"

"I want to know how you got the answer key," Mr. Keeler demands. "I wrote the test on Monday evening, and only my first and second period classes would have seen it before you took the test. Who shared the questions with you?"

I roll my eyes. "Hello? I studied. It's not a hard concept, people. Aren't you always saying that studying is the only way to get good grades?" I look at Mom, who's just sitting there between Ms. Detweiler and Mr. Keeler, staring at her shoes. "Tell them about the way Dave's been tutoring me."

Everyone turns their attention to Mom, and she shifts uncomfortably in her seat. "Well, David has been coming over every night for the past two weeks," she says. "And I assumed they were studying. Andrea's grades have certainly improved. I was just telling her father that I couldn't be more proud of her progress." She hesitates. "But there is an awful lot of giggling going on in these study sessions. I don't recall biology being so amusing."

I throw my hands up. "Seriously? Dave's funny. He makes biology interesting. Maybe if Mr. Keeler wasn't so freaking boring, people could learn something in class, too, and we wouldn't have to hire tutors to pass."

Mr. Keeler glares at me, and I fold my arms across my chest, glaring right back at him.

"Maybe she could retake the test?" Mom asks. "A different version to prove that she didn't cheat?" She smiles and nods, as if this solves everything. But I totally don't see why I should be punished. Why should I have to take another test, just because my biology teacher's a jerk?

Mr. Keeler snorts. "I don't give retakes."

Mom looks from me to Mr. Keeler and back again. "What if she's innocent? Would you deny her the grade she earned?"

Mr. Keeler crosses his arms and scowls at me. "She earned a zero. Cheating should never be rewarded."

Ms. Detweiler and Mrs. Gardner look like a couple of deer caught in the headlights, and Mom's best argument is "What if she didn't cheat?"

Obviously, it's up to me to fix things.

"Whatever," I say. "I totally deserve at least one

hundred percent, even if you won't give me credit for the bonus questions. If you don't believe I studied, try me. I can prove it right now." I pull my biology textbook out of my bag and hand it to Ms. Detweiler. I toss my notebook into my backpack and slide the whole thing across the room to Mr. Keeler, and then I roll up my sleeves to show my bare arms and hands. I point to the textbook. "If Mr. Keeler asks totally random questions that he pulls out on the spot, there's no way I could memorize the answers in advance, right? I'll only pass if I really know this crap."

Mom inhales sharply. "Watch your language sweetie," she whispers.

Ms. Detweiler nods. "That seems fair. Mr. Keeler, please ask a series of five questions to randomly sample the material on your exam. If Ms. Andersen can get them all right, you'll give her full credit for her perfect score on the exam, including the bonus question, plus extra credit for the impromptu pop quiz." She looks at me. "I have no doubt you studied. However, since the question here is not whether you can pass the test, but whether you've studied enough to be the first student ever to get every single question right, this is an all-or-nothing situation. If you miss a single answer, the zero stands and we'll talk about honor code disciplinary measures. Does this seem fair?"

I toss my hair and smirk. "Bring it." It's totally unfair, and I'm afraid I'll make a stupid mistake and miss some super-easy question, but there's no way I'm backing down now. Teachers can smell fear. If I even hesitate or show that I'm nervous, they'll all take it as proof that I cheated.

Mr. Keeler nods and opens the book, glaring at me over the pages.

"What is Mendel's law of segregation?"

Yeah, I should've known he would go for the hardest questions possible. Luckily, Dave spent over an hour explaining this one to me. I describe Mendel's experiments with the pea plants and how he discovered that each offspring receives one gene from each parent.

"What are alleles?"

"What does it mean to be co-dominant?"

"What does it mean to be homozygous?"

"What does heterozygous mean?"

I answer each question without missing a beat. This is easier than I thought it would be.

Mr. Keeler scowls and flips through the textbook again. He grabs a piece of paper off of Ms. Detweiler's desk and shoves it at me. "Draw a Punnett square diagram of how alleles for freckles would be distributed if you have two heterozygous parents."

I cross my arms and shake my head. "You were only supposed to ask five questions. This makes six."

"No." he shoves the paper at me again. "The definitions were all part of one question. I've only asked two. But if this is getting too hard for you, you're welcome to admit that you cheated."

I grab the paper from him and snatch a pen off Ms. Detweiler's desk. "You're totally cheating, Mr. Keeler, but whatever," I mutter. I draw the table he asked for, even though he didn't give me all the information I need.

Luckily, I remember that the trait for freckles is dominant and the one for no freckles is recessive, thanks to Dave's teasing me about my face full of freckles when he was helping me study. I hold up the paper, for everyone to see and smile at Mr. Keeler. "You'd get a one-fourth chance of getting a child homozygous for freckles, one-fourth chance of a child homozygous without freckles, and two-fourths chance for a child that is heterozygous, like the parents. And in case you're wondering, all of those heterozygous people would have butt loads of freckles." I toss the paper back at him.

"And that makes six questions, doesn't it?" Mom asks. "The question about segregation, the four different definitions, and this diagram."

"Yes, I believe you're right, Mrs. Andersen," Ms. Detweiler says. "And I think we've seen enough. Mr. Keeler, you owe Ms. Andersen an apology."

He coughs and splutters. "The definitions were all sub points of one question. I still have two more."

Ms. Detweiler frowns. "No, I believe we have sufficient proof that Ms. Andersen earned her grade. And perhaps we should have a discussion about showing mutual respect for our students, after Ms. Andersen returns to class."

Mom grins and steps across the room to hug me. "You handled that well," she says. "I knew my daughter would never cheat."

Right. Because she totally didn't try to throw me under the bus with that "I don't remember biology being so humorous" line. But I smile and nod and return her hug. I still need her on my side, if I plan to continue with *Cinderella*.

Ms. Detweiler shakes my hand. "Well done, Andi. I'd say your tutoring sessions have been quite successful." She looks at Mom. "It appears that Alaina isn't your only brilliant daughter, Mrs. Andersen."

Mrs. Gardner squeezes my arm affectionately. "I believe I have another student waiting to speak with me," she says, "so if I'm no longer needed here?"

Ms. Detweiler nods and Mrs. Gardner leaves.

Mr. Keeler slams my textbook closed and tosses it onto my chair. "If my tests are so easy, Ms. Andersen, I expect to see you getting one hundred percent on every quiz and exam from now on."

"Count on it." I shove my book into my backpack and turn to Ms. Detweiler. "Can I go back to class now?"

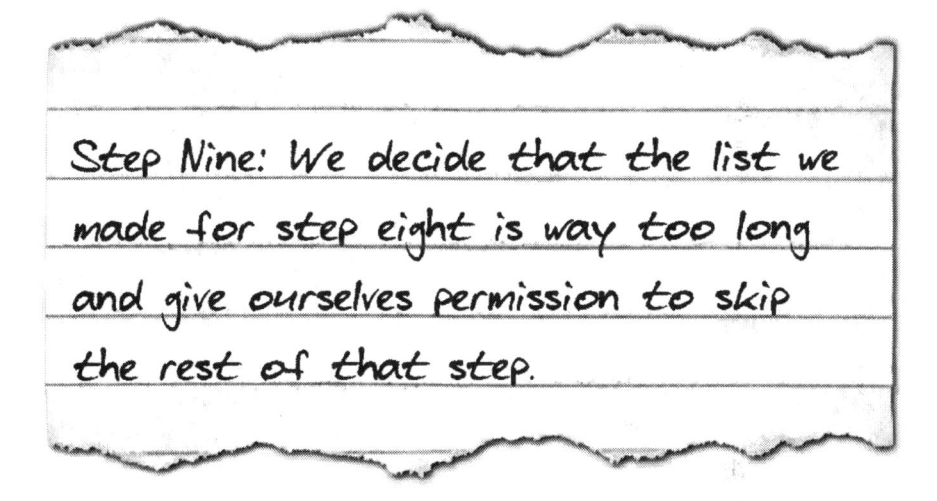

Step Nine: We decide that the list we made for step eight is way too long and give ourselves permission to skip the rest of that step.

Step Ten: We continue to take personal offense when someone compares us to our perfect siblings. (It may not be the healthiest step, but hey, at least we're being honest!)

Chapter Thirty

I peek through the curtain at the crowd filling the auditorium. The house is packed, but I'm not even close to nervous. The butterflies in my stomach flutter low with anticipation, but not fear. I turn away from the curtain to watch my fellow cast members hurrying around backstage. A million things went wrong in our final dress rehearsal last night, but Jarod says that the rule is a bad dress rehearsal leads to a good performance. It totally doesn't make sense, but he's been through way more opening nights than I have, and I believe him.

We're going to totally rock this thing.

The house lights go down and Cara takes her place, center stage, for the first scene. As the curtain rises and the spotlights highlight the world Dave and the rest of the stage crew have created, I slip out of myself and become Arika, Cinderella's sexy stepsister who might actually have a chance with Prince Charming.

Jarod squeezes my hand and smiles at me as he passes by on his way to meet the poor waif, Cinderella, as a weary traveler, looking for a drink of water. The butterflies in my stomach start flapping like crazy when he touches me, and then they die in a churning, bubbling fire as I watch my prince flirting with the sweet, innocent Cinderella in her garden. Even dressed in rags and with makeup smudged like dirt on her cheeks, Cara's prettier than I am. I can totally see why Cinderella's stepsisters were mean to her. It sucks to be completely overlooked and ignored while everyone on the planet practically worships your sister.

When I hear my cue, I drift onstage behind Rebekah and Kathy to knock Cinderella down a few pegs. "You really think the Prince would want someone like you?" I sneer, letting loose every ounce of frustration I feel. "The Prince may not yet know what he wants, but seriously, you're not his type."

Rebekah giggles nervously, not sure of what to do with my ad-libbed lines, but Kathy jumps right in. "Yes, Cinderella. Stop this foolish dreaming and lay out our dresses at once. You must help my daughters prepare for the ball. One of them is certain to catch the Prince's eye this evening."

We flounce offstage and Mrs. Mason hugs me. "You were brilliant," she gushes. "That little extra bit was perfect foreshadowing for the ballroom scene later. Andi, you're a natural,"

I float through the performance in a semi-daze as I allow Arika to fully inhabit my body, and before I know it, we're lined up onstage for our final bows. Jarod and Cara, Prince Charming and Cinderella, step forward, hand-in-hand, waving and smiling at the audience. Then, Jarod drops Cara's hand and reaches back to pull me into the spotlight. The audience erupts in a series of cheers and whistles, and I curtsy awkwardly. "It's not often that the stepsister steals the show," Jarod whispers, "but I'm not surprised. You're amazing."

Dave is waiting in the wings to congratulate me with a giant bouquet of daisies. "Wow. That was incredible."

I take the flowers and breathe deeply. "Thanks. They're beautiful. How did you know daisies are my favorite?"

He grins. "I told you. I pay attention."

Jarod slips an arm around my waist and pulls me over to a small table next to the costume rack outside the dressing rooms. "These are for you." He takes the daisy bouquet out of my hands and replaces it with a giant bouquet of pink roses. "The most beautiful girl at the ball."

"Thanks." There must be two dozen roses here. So what if they're not my favorite? He didn't have to get anything for me. And a giant bouquet like this probably cost a lot. So I hide my disappointment behind a giant smile and give Jarod a hug. It's not his fault that he thinks Laina's not the only Andersen sister who loves pink roses.

"Will you come with me to the after-party?" Jarod asks.

I step back and look into his green eyes. "Are you sure? There will be a lot of people. And they might see us together."

"I don't care. Let them see."

I've been waiting for years for Jarod to choose me, but somehow I expected it to feel more satisfying. I glance over my shoulder to where Dave was standing a minute ago, but he's already gone. I push aside a flutter of disappointment and take a deep breath, filling my nose with the sweet perfume of roses. Jarod is the one who wants me, not Dave. And that's what I've always wanted.

I meet Jarod's expectant gaze with a smile. "Yes."

I step into his arms and tip my face up for a kiss, but Jarod isn't looking at me anymore. He's staring past me with a dreamy look in his eyes. I follow his gaze, and my heart plummets. "Hi, Laina. What did you think of the performance?"

"Oh my gosh, you guys, that was amazing. Jarod, who knew you would look so good in tights?" She rushes over and throws her arms around him, squealing in delight.

He blushes and tugs down on the hem of his tunic. "Well, you know, they're incredibly comfortable. I think we should bring the whole Renaissance look back in style." He points at me over his shoulder, without taking his eyes off her. "We were just getting ready to go to the cast party. Do you want to come with us?"

"Oh, I couldn't. I'm not part of the cast. And I look atrocious." She brushes her hand over the bulky sweater she's wearing and bites her lip, waiting for us to contradict her.

Of course she knows she looks amazing. She always looks amazing. And I'm not really in the mood to play feed-Laina's-ego tonight.

"No way. You're gorgeous," Jarod says. "And we're allowed to bring guests to the party. You can come with me and Andi."

They wander away, discussing the pros and cons of corsets and tunics, and I quietly fade into the background. Neither of them even notices that I've disappeared. Because no matter how much you tweak the script, the Prince will always pick Cinderella.

No one wants her sister.

I find my parents in the lobby and convince them that I'm not feeling well. I'd rather go to bed early than suffer through another party as Jarod and Laina's third wheel.

The crowded backstage area buzzes with excitement as I walk into the theater. Last night's opening performance was amazing, and I can tell I'm not the only one still high on a rush of adrenaline.

"We killed it last night," Rebekah says, hugging me. "This is going to be a great run,"

"Did you see your review?" Kathy asks, handing me a copy of the local newspaper with a giant picture of me and Jarod on the front page. "Congratulations, sweetie. They love you." She hugs me and rushes off before I have a chance to answer.

Of course I've read it. Mom had a stack of newspapers a mile high sitting on the kitchen counter when I woke up this morning. She's probably still on the phone, calling everyone she knows to brag about it.

Even Laina's never been on the front page of the newspaper.

Several cast members stop me to offer congratulations as I make my way over to the costume rack to grab my gown for the opening scene.

A wilted bouquet of daisies glares at me from the table, where I left them last night. Did I even remember to thank Dave for the flowers?

I pick them up to smell the wilted blossoms, and my chest tightens when I see a note tucked in among the limp stems. "I'd choose the sexy stepsister over Cinderella any day." Maybe Dave doesn't just want to be friends. Maybe I completely misread his signals. Maybe it's not too late for my own happily ever after.

"I didn't see you at the party last night." Dave appears beside me and lifts the dead flowers from my arms. He turns his back on me and studies the limp, brown petals.

"Yeah, I was kind of sick," I say. "I went to bed early." I'm glad he's not looking at me, because I can't hide the blush creeping into my cheeks.

He shakes his head and pulls the petals off the biggest daisy, one by one, dropping them to the floor haphazardly. "There must be something going around. Prince Charming didn't show up at the party either. Hope you're not both too sick to perform today." He doesn't look at me.

I swallow the lump in my throat. "I wasn't with Jarod. I went to bed." And Laina didn't come home until nearly midnight. "Thank you for the flowers. They were beautiful."

Dave dumps the daisies into the trash and shrugs. "Yeah, well, daisies can't compete with roses."

"Dave, I ..."

He sighs. "You'd better go get into costume. Mrs. Mason wants to talk to the whole cast before the audience arrives. Go over a few little hiccups from last night. And I've got work to do." He waves his hand toward the empty stage. "I'm missing three props and we're still having issues with the backdrop for the garden scene." He walks away, mumbling about inconsiderate actors as he throws away a handful of discarded napkins and empty coffee cups from the floor.

I totally screwed up when I ditched him for Jarod last night.

And I deserved it when Jarod ditched me for Laina.

Grabbing my costume for the first act from the rack, I turn and start toward the women's dressing room. At least I don't have to keep wondering if I have a chance with Jarod. He made it perfectly clear last night which sister he wants. If only I'd realized that I didn't want him either before I blew my last chance with Dave.

I trip over a pumpkin and nearly fall flat on my face, but strong arms wrap around my waist from behind, steadying me.

"You okay?" Jarod turns me around to face him.

"I'm fine. Just clumsy."

He brushes a loose strand of hair out of my face. "No, that's not what I mean. Your dad said you were feeling sick last night. And you ran off without even telling me where you were going. We had a date, remember?" He smiles. "Are you okay now?"

Maybe Jarod wasn't trying to ditch me for Laina. What

if he just wanted to prove that he wasn't hiding anymore? Would it even matter?

"Yeah, I'm fine." I glance across the stage to where Dave is wrestling with the garden backdrop that keeps leaning to the left. How had I never noticed that Dave had painted a whole garden full of daisies? "I need to go get dressed, but I'll see you onstage in a bit, okay?"

Jarod nods and kisses my cheek, and I sprint to the dressing room, questions swirling in my mind.

I always thought daisies were my favorite flower. They're uncomplicated and straightforward, and you always know exactly what you're getting. But I never really had to choose between roses and daisies before.

I peek through the curtains at the crowd filling the auditorium. Mom and Dad are sitting in the middle of the fourth row, as always. They've been here for every single show, even missing church for last Sunday's matinee. Tonight, Dad invited his boss, bragging about me the way he's always bragging about Laina.

"Wow," Nathaniel leans over my shoulder to get a better look. "Who's the chick with the boobs out there talking to Jarod?" He's practically salivating as he ogles Laina.

"That's my sister, you creep. And you don't have a chance with her, so don't even think about it."

He smirks at my non-existent chest. "Guess the hot body genes skipped a generation, huh? Must be why Jarod likes the ballroom scene. That boob-lift dress you wear makes you look stacked."

"We're sisters. That's the same generation, dipweed." I

spin on my heel and stalk off to the dressing room.

Is that really the only thing Jarod sees in me? I always felt so pretty and princessy in my ball gown, but now I don't even want to wear it. I slap on my stage makeup and pull my hair up into the elaborate stepsister hairstyle. I examine myself in the mirror and take a deep breath. Jarod kissed me long before I was cast as the stepsister. It's not all costume magic. But was I ever anything more than a stand-in for Laina?

I'm glad this is our last performance, because I don't think I could take one more night with Duke Dipweed. He's rude and inconsiderate, and maybe even completely right.

Emily wanted me to ditch the show tonight, because Nick's throwing his annual my-parents-went-out-of-town-for-their-anniversary party. And maybe I should have gone with her. My understudy could have handled this last performance, and I'm tired of trying to be someone I'm not.

But Dad invited his freaking boss. He's never invited his boss to anything, even last year, when Laina had three different solos in the spring concert. I couldn't exactly skip this.

I run through the first act on autopilot, but when Prince Charming sweeps me into his arms for our big dance, he whispers "You look beautiful tonight," and I let myself get carried away into the fantasy. I smile and laugh my way through the rehearsed banter that's supposed to make the audience wonder who the Prince will ultimately choose.

Until I catch Jarod staring at my boobs.

"Hey, Prince Not-So-Charming, I'm up here." I lift his chin so that his eyes meet mine. "The melons aren't gonna talk, bud." I stop dancing and twist out of his arms. "If you're only looking for a pair of boobs, you might want to try my sister, because I have way more to offer than that."

I stomp offstage as Cara makes her grand entrance, leaving Rebekah to sing our duet alone. Luckily, she can sing both parts perfectly, and there's a pretty good chance that most people in the audience haven't seen the earlier performances, so they probably think my outburst is part of the script.

I hope.

Mrs. Mason quickly calls Rebekah and Kathy over for a conference while Jarod and Cara profess their undying love for each other onstage.

"Andi, I love the feminist take on the ballroom scene," Mrs. Mason says, "but I wish you'd run it past me in rehearsals instead of throwing it out there for the very first time during our final performance."

I stare at the floor between my shoes. "Yeah. Sorry about that."

"I thought it was awesome," Rebekah says, peeking around the curtain. "And it definitely got the audience's attention."

Mrs. Mason smiles. "I thought it was kind of awesome, too. I only wish we'd thought of it sooner. But we'll need to tweak the rest of the script a bit to make it fit." She glances at the stage, where Cara is about to run away from Prince Charming, leaving her glass slipper behind. "Who would have guessed Cinderella caught the Prince on the rebound?"

After a quick set and costume change, Cara wanders back "home" in her old rags and sings a reprise of her song about daydreaming. When she finishes the song, I emerge from behind a partition, as if coming into the kitchen from another room in the house. "Where have you been?" I demand. "I had to untie the laces on that wretched ball gown all by myself."

Cara's eyes widen. Of course, she has no idea what's going on, because she was with Prince Charming while we were frantically rewriting the script, but she plays along perfectly. "I was in the garden. Dreaming of the Prince," she says with a sigh. "And it was the most lovely night."

Rebekah and Kathy join us onstage, gushing about the

ball and complaining about the mystery girl who stole Prince Charming's heart.

"She can have him," I say. "That prince is anything but charming."

"Oh, no," Cara gushes. "He's kind and gentle." She glances at us, a convincing look of terror on her face. "At least, that is how I imagine him."

They transition easily into the song where the stepsisters and stepmother compare their impressions of the ball with Cinderella's "dream" of what it was like. Rebekah sings my lines while I mutter insults under my breath.

When Prince Charming and his servant come to try the glass slipper, Kathy and Rebekah trip all over themselves to get a chance, like the original script says. But when it's my turn to try, I shake my head. "Nah, I'm good, thanks," I say, and the audience roars. I can't help smirking when I see the way Jarod blushes.

When the play is over and we line up to take our final bows, Jarod and Cara step forward to receive applause as the stars of the show. When Jarod reaches back to take my hand, as he has after every performance, I step around him to take a bow on my own, and the entire audience leaps up to give me a standing ovation. Even through the bright stage lights, I can see Dad whispering excitedly to his boss. I smile and wave and blow a few kisses before I walk offstage, without waiting for the final bow. I shoot Jarod a nasty look over my shoulder, and I'm pretty sure everyone thinks I'm still playing the part.

But he knows it's real, and that's what really matters.

I rush to the dressing room and change into my street clothes, and then I call Nick while I scrub off the stage makeup. He agrees to come and pick me up, and I slip out into the back parking lot to wait for him, as the rest of the cast streams offstage.

Chapter Thirty-One

As soon as we get to Nick's house, I head straight for the kitchen and grab a red, plastic cup full of something green and fruity. I down it in one long gulp, ignoring the burn in my throat, and reach for another.

"Whoa," Nick says, coming up behind me. "Pace yourself. That stuff's kind of strong."

I finish off the second cup and then reach for a beer. "I don't need a babysitter. I can handle myself." I'm tired of trying to show the world that I can be as good as Laina. I'm her sister, not her shadow.

Nick shakes his head and backs off. "Take it easy, okay? You don't need to prove anything."

"Whatever." I walk away, already feeling lighter as the fruity punch works its magic. I've been so focused on trying to be like my sister that I haven't been to a party in months. But this is who I am. I'm fun and bubbly and carefree, and I may not be some perfect, plastic doll, but I'm freaking awesome.

And anyone who can't accept me for who I am—

I trip on the rug in the hallway and fall against Josh, spilling the last of my beer on his t-shirt. "Whoops! Sorry, Joshie." I pat his cheek and grin.

He grabs my shoulders to steady me. "Hey, Andi, what's up? I haven't seen you in a while."

"Yeah, well, I've been busy." I step away from him, flip my hair over my shoulder and lean casually against the wall.

Except, someone moved the doorway.

I stumble backward into the living room and trip over a table. A lamp crashes to the floor, but luckily, the carpet is soft enough to keep it from shattering. The crack on the base was probably even there already.

I put the lamp back on the table and giggle. The best way to get over an embarrassing moment is to pretend it's no big deal, so I don't even try to make excuses for my klutziness. I wander over to the couch and wedge myself in between Rob and some random guy.

Someone hands me another beer and I pop the top and take a long drink. "Hey, Robbie, whatcha doin'?"

"Well, hello," says random guy. "I don't think we've met."

"Nope." I try to take another swig of my drink, but the can is empty. How did that happen?

"I'm Max," random guy says. "And you are?"

"Exhausted." I lean my head back against the couch cushions and close my eyes to wait for the room to stop spinning.

Maybe I should've eased back into the whole party thing. Even back when I used to come to these parties every weekend, I didn't actually drink much. I used to carry around the same can of beer all night long.

It's a great prop. If you're holding a drink in your hand, you can usually say or do whatever you want, and if it comes out stupid, you have a built-in excuse. You can get away with anything as long as you say, "I was so drunk, I don't even remember what happened!" Even if you haven't had a single sip yet.

But tonight, I may actually be a teensy bit tipsy.

I giggle. "Tipsy is a funny word, isn't it? Tipsy, tipsy, tipsy."

"This is Andi," Rob says to random guy. "She's Alaina Andersen's little sister."

"Alaina?"

"Yeah. She sits behind me in chemistry. Killer body."

"Oh, you mean that chick with the boobs and the long hair? The one that's always writing in that notebook? She's hot."

I open my eyes and push myself off the couch without waiting to hear Rob's reply. I'm tired of hearing about the amazing Alaina Andersen. I wander back down the hall, trying to remember where the bathroom is.

Because I think I need to pee.

And maybe throw up.

I leave the main crowd of people and climb over the bookshelf Nick has blocking the stairs. He never lets anyone up on the second floor, because his mom doesn't care about his not-so-secret parties as long as he keeps everyone out of the bedrooms. But I happen to know there are three bathrooms upstairs with no lines, and my bladder doesn't want to wait.

After I pee and wash my hands, I splash my face with cold water. The nauseous feeling leaves, and I go back downstairs to find Nick.

I'm ready to leave, because this party kind of sucks, but Nick isn't in the living room or the kitchen. I'm totally dehydrated, so I grab another cup of punch on my way out to the back yard to look for him.

It's not nearly as crowded out here as it is inside the house, and it's easy to find Nick. He's sitting on top of the picnic table, surrounded by a flock of admiring sophomore and freshman girls, who are hanging on his every word and acting like he's some sort of god.

I'm pretty sure this is the reason Nick throws his parties. He loves having a flock of admirers. And he probably won't want to leave them again so soon. I already made him ditch the party once, to come pick me up. I'll have to find someone else who isn't too sloshed to take me home.

Shane sits on a bench on the opposite side of the porch, talking to Adam. Kendra's draped across Shane's lap, kissing his neck and running her fingers through his hair, but he's completely ignoring her, except when he pushes her hands away, like he's trying to get rid of an annoying fly. I'm willing to bet she's barely had anything to drink, but come Monday morning, she'll be blaming her totally drunken state if anyone says anything about the way she's acting.

It's too bad Laina never comes to these parties. Maybe she'd finally believe me when I say her best friend is a total witch.

I walk back into the kitchen and bump into Rob and random guy next to the punch bowl. "Hey, little sister," random guy says. He raises his plastic cup in greeting and I nod. "You know, you may not have a body like your sister, but you're not half-bad." He grabs my boob with his free hand and squeezes. "I'd get with this."

I kick him, hard, and when he lets go of me and doubles over in pain, I grab his drink and dump it over his head. "You're an idiot."

I refill my cup and stomp away.

Rob follows me out of the kitchen. "That was awesome. Remind me never to get on your bad side, Alaina."

I stop walking and spin around. "I'm not Laina, Rob. I'm nothing like her."

He studies me for a minute. "I don't know. You're sisters, right? So you're kind of alike." He shrugs. "Max is a dick, but he's not wrong. You're kind of hot."

"Kind of?" I set my cup on a nearby table and flash my sexiest smile at him. I run my fingers across his abs and then slide my hands up his body, pushing him backward until he's pressed up against the wall. He's breathing heavily by the time I tip my face up toward his and capture his bottom lip with my teeth. I slide my hands up to tangle in his hair, and lean into him, pressing my body against his as the kiss deepens.

Rob wraps his arms around my waist, and then his hands slowly drift downward. He pulls me into him, thrusting his hips forward and grinding against me. He moans softly as I plant tiny kisses along his jawline. When my lips reach his ear, I pause for a moment, letting him go crazy with wanting me.

He groans and turns his face, trying to recapture my lips.

"I'm more than kind of hot, loser," I say. Then I spin out of his arms, grab my cup, and walk away without a backward glance. Other than the tiny bit where I stumble against the wall, it's a perfect exit.

Screw this. I'm so ready to go home, it's not even funny. I don't care how busy Nick is. I march back outside to grab him, but the picnic table is empty. Nick and his harem must've migrated inside.

But Shane and the Witch are still sitting on the bench.

"Come on, lover boy," I say. "I need a ride home, and you're it."

He stands up, pushing Kendra off his lap, and pulls his keys out of his pocket. "No problem. I wanted to talk to you anyway. Alaina's kind of avoiding me."

"Um, yeah, if you want to get with my sister, letting her best friend paw you in public probably isn't the best way to do it." I grab his hand and start to walk around the house to the cars parked out on the street.

"Excuse me, but we're kind of in the middle of something here," Kendra says. She yanks our hands apart and steps between us, glaring at me with her arms folded. "If you're too trashed to get yourself home, go find some other loser to drive you. Shane's busy."

"Nah, this loser is fine," I say. "And it looks to me like he's only busy trying to get rid of you. C'mon Shane, let's go."

I turn and start walking to the car, but Kendra shoves me from behind, and I fall flat on my face. "You're pathetic," she sneers. "Using your sister as an excuse to get a guy to talk to you. Even Alaina isn't that desperate."

I roll over and pull myself up. "Oh, please. Save the drama. I'm not the one throwing myself at a guy who's obviously not interested. You may have my sister fooled, but everyone else can see that you're totally using her."

"I don't need to take this from you." She slaps my face and takes a deep breath, preparing to let loose with one of her famous I'm-so-much-better-than-you speeches. But I've had enough crap tonight. I punch her in the nose, and she crumples to the ground to a chorus of cheers from the crowd of kids who had gathered in the yard to watch the show.

"So are you gonna give me a ride or not?" I ask. Shane nods and jingles his keys, stepping around Kendra and leading the way to his car.

But we've only taken a few steps before Dave steps out of the crowd. "You've been drinking," he says, holding out his hand for the keys. "No way I'm letting you behind the wheel with Andi in the car. I'll drive you both home."

My head is pounding and it tastes like something died in my

mouth. I don't remember getting home last night, and I wonder how Dave got me past Mom and Dad.

He must have managed somehow, because I'm not dead.

Someone left a glass of water and a couple of ibuprofen on my nightstand, and I swallow them gratefully before sinking back into bed and pulling my pillow over my head to block the sunlight streaming in through the window.

"Rise and shine, sweetie!" Mom barges into my room and pulls my pillow away. "It's almost time for church." Her voice is honey-sweet and dripping sunshine, but I can tell by the look in her eyes that Dave didn't sneak me past her last night after all.

"I'm sick." I cough weakly, but the effect is ruined when I moan and grab my head to stop the throbbing.

She holds her hand to my forehead in mock concern, and then she shakes her head. "Nope. No fever. You'll feel better when you're up and moving." She reaches over me and turns on my radio, full volume. "There. Some nice, cheery music is all you need to get you going this morning." She grins and grabs my arms to pull me into a sitting position. Then, she glares at me, daring me to challenge her. I turn off the radio and swing my legs off the edge of the bed.

"I'll be ready in ten minutes."

She nods and walks to the door. "I'm glad you're feeling better," she says. "Mother's Day services wouldn't be the same if I didn't have both of my girls at church with me."

Crap!

I was supposed to help Laina make a surprise breakfast as our Mother's Day present.

Mom shuts the door, harder than she'd ever allow me to, and I cringe. I wait for the room to stop spinning and then I drag myself to the closet. I pull out the pink, gauzy dress that Mom gave me for Christmas.

I hate this dress. It makes me feel like a little girl,

playing princess dress-up. But Mom thought the little blue flowers embroidered on the collar and along the hem would bring out my eyes. And I know it hurt her feelings when I refused to wear it.

I snip off the tags and pull the dress over my head. Hopefully, when Mom sees me, she'll know I'm sorry about ruining her Mother's Day.

I grab my hairbrush and run it through my hair as I turn to the mirror hanging above my desk. And I freeze, mid-stroke. Sitting in the center of my desk, right between my biology textbook and my math notebook, is the biggest bouquet of daisies I've ever seen. Dave must have put them here when he brought me home last night.

I drop the brush and reach for the card.

"Andi, we're so proud of you. Congratulations on a great run as the best stepsister in the history of *Cinderella*. Love, Mom and Dad."

The whole family is waiting for me in the kitchen by the time I drag myself out of my bedroom.

"There she is!" Dad booms. "Our little princess looks sleepy this morning. Maybe she'll think twice about staying out past curfew in the future." He laughs loudly and slams a cabinet door. "You missed breakfast, pumpkin, but I made you a plate. You can bring it with us." The smell of waffles and strawberries nearly knocks me over, and I swallow hard, fighting the urge to vomit.

"That's okay. I'm not really hungry." I kiss Mom on the cheek and hand her the card I bought. "Happy Mother's Day. And thank you for the flowers."

I follow my family out to the car, ignoring the daggers Laina's staring into me, and close my eyes against the bright sunshine. Unfortunately, I can't do anything about the crash of music Dad decides to blast through the stereo, even though he always says loud music makes it impossible to prepare for Sabbath worship.

Jarod's standing in the foyer when we walk into church. "Happy Mother's Day, Mrs. Andersen," he says and hands Mom a pink carnation. Then, he shakes hands with Dad.

My parents beam at Jarod. "Good morning."

Dad winks at Laina, who blushes like crazy. Then he takes Mom's hand and they walk into the chapel.

Jarod hugs me. "I'm sorry. I've been a jerk. And you deserve more." He looks over my shoulder, at Laina. "You know you're one of my best friends, right? I never wanted to hurt you."

He blushes when Laina smiles at him.

"Yeah, I understand," I say. Because that's the appropriate response at a time like this. It's in the script. And my head hurts too much to come up with anything better.

Jarod grins. "You're the best."

I nod, and he walks across the room to join Laina.

I wait for the familiar twinge to wrench my stomach, but it doesn't come. Between the throbbing headache and the nausea, I don't have the energy to care.

Laina laughs at something Jarod says, and he kisses her cheek before walking into the chapel to join his parents.

"So," I say, grinning as I loop my arm through Laina's, "you and Jarod are official now?"

Laina snorts. "We're not dating. That would ruin everything. We're buds." She frowns and pulls her arm away. "And I'm still not speaking to you. Do you know how hard it was to make Mom's entire breakfast all by myself?"

I bat my eyelashes innocently and lean my head on her shoulder in the perfect puppy dog pout. "I'm sorry, Laina. I was stupid. But it's not like I would've been much help anyway. You're the chef of the family, and we all know it." I stick out my bottom lip. "I would've burned the waffles and messed it all up."

Laina rolls her eyes and pulls me into the chapel. "Come on, drama queen. At least have the courtesy not to make us late for church." She frowns and shakes her head, but I see a tiny twinkle in her eye, and I know she's already forgiven me.

Miss Perfect doesn't hold grudges.

Step Eleven: We seek, through study and preparation, to improve our grades and overall reputations, desiring to be recognized for our own accomplishments and not as mere shadows of our perfect siblings.

Chapter Thirty-Two

"Hey, sexy lady!" Some vaguely familiar guy yells across the commons area as I walk into school. "You disappeared before we got a chance to get to know each other at Nick's party." He jogs over. "Wanna pick up where we left off?"

I take a step back and smile hesitantly as I attempt to remember Saturday night.

"Give it up, Max," Dave says. He slips an arm around my waist possessively. "And leave my girlfriend alone."

Max shrugs. "It's your loss, Andi. If you want to stick with a loser like this when you could have a real man, that's your choice."

He walks away, shaking his head in disbelief, and I turn to look at Dave. "I'm your girlfriend?"

Dave smiles and releases me. "I figured I'd help you out with Max. He's not really a bad guy, but he doesn't always know when to give up. And he's not your type. Trust me."

"Right. So, thanks, I guess." I hug my books to my chest and fight the urge to run my fingers through Dave's hair to straighten his messy curls. "Oh, and thanks for being my knight in shining armor again."

"Well, rescuing damsels in distress is kind of a hobby of mine."

I take his hand and we walk to first period together. "You could totally be a professional damsel rescuer. As long as I get to be first in line for help."

"It's a deal. But next time you flip out and go insane, would you please call me first? I wouldn't have even known where you were if Nick hadn't texted me to come get you."

I pull away. "I told him I could take care of myself."

"I found you in the middle of a drunken cat fight with Kendra Smith, and you were so wasted that you didn't even get to my car before passing out. And I didn't get to witness your grope-fest with Rob, but I heard all about it from Max and Josh. Yeah. You can totally take care of yourself." He shakes his head. "Nick was worried, and you wouldn't listen to him, so he called me."

"Whatever. I had everything under control. And Kendra deserved it."

Dave stops outside the classroom door, blocking my path. "That wasn't you. You're better than that."

"I'm not Laina, you know. Some of us aren't perfect."

"I know. But that girl at the party? That wasn't you."

I push past him and into the classroom as the tardy bell rings. Mr. Mayer slaps a pink slip of paper onto my desk as I sit down. "Third tardy this month, Ms. Andersen," he says. "Looks like I have a date for lunch. Bring something chocolate, because I need to maintain my girlish figure." He pats his bulging stomach, earning giggles from the other kids in class. Then, he glances toward the door as Dave saunters in. "That makes two for you, Mr. Maestas. In the future, I'd suggest that you finish your canoodling on your own time, or you'll be joining your girlfriend for lunchtime detention, and there's nothing romantic about a hot lunch date with your boring, old history teacher."

"Aww, c'mon, Mr. Mayer," Nick calls from the back of the room. "You're not that old."

Everyone laughs and Mr. Mayer grins. "Okay, now. Let's settle down and get to work, shall we? I'll try not to be too boring."

Dave nods and blushes as he slips into his seat. I can feel his eyes burning into me, but I refuse to look at him. Emily slips a folded piece of paper onto my desk, which I carefully open as soon as Mr. Mayer turns his attention to his lecture notes.

"What happened to you this weekend? I thought you were gonna call me after the play." I roll my eyes in an "it's a long story, I'll tell you about it later" kind of way. She'll probably hear the whole story by lunchtime anyway.

Summer tosses her purse on the back seat and smiles. "Welcome back to the real world, Andi. No more play practices or dance rehearsals. Let's go celebrate!"

"Any excuse to go shopping, huh?" I laugh and stretch my legs across the back seat.

"Well, now that you mention it, I saw the cutest top at Hot Couture last week. You have to get it. You'll look adorable."

Emily sighs and adjusts the volume on the radio. "She always looks adorable. She doesn't need a bunch of new clothes to prove it." She turns to look at me. "Besides, aren't you grounded? I heard your parents were still awake when

Dave brought you home Saturday night. They must've been pissed."

I shrug. "I'm sure I will be soon, but they still haven't actually given me my punishment. I got the standard we-taught-you-better-than-this lecture yesterday, but nothing really happened."

"Really?" Emily giggles. "You truly are the master manipulator, aren't you? Nothing ever sticks to you."

"I'm pretty sure they're drawing it out on purpose," I say, "waiting for me to crack. You should have seen me yesterday, tiptoeing around possible landmines, waiting for them to explode. This waiting is worse than any punishment they could come up with."

Summer frowns. "Are they gonna kill you if you don't come straight home? I don't want to make it worse."

"No. I need to get out. I'm exhausted. Besides, nothing they do to me could possibly be worse than the day I've had."

I wanted to show the world that I'm nothing like my sister, but it completely backfired. People are comparing me to Laina more than ever. And not in a good way.

Dave and Nick were right. That totally wasn't me on Saturday night, and I don't even have anything to show for it, unless you count the "When Drunk Girls Attack" video someone posted online.

I totally need some time out with my best friends before I'm stuck in solitary confinement for the rest of my life.

The top Summer found last week isn't nearly as cute as she remembered. We spend the next two hours browsing the racks at every decent store in the mall without finding anything. And I've lost track of how many times I've heard girls whispering "Is that Laina's sister? How are they even related?" or "Alaina must be so embarrassed."

By the time we stop for smoothies in the food court, I'm beyond ready to be done with this whole day.

"Hey, Andi, what's up?" Rob appears out of nowhere and grabs my butt. "I'm done with work. Want to go somewhere?"

I smack his hand away. "Nope. I'm hangin' out with my friends."

"How about after? I'm free for the rest of the night." He grins and reaches for me again.

"Go away, Rob. I'm not interested." I sidestep his grabby hands and turn my attention back to my friends. He had zero interest in me before, but now he suddenly thinks I'm irresistible? Um, yeah, no thanks. He wasn't even a very good kisser.

I finally convince Summer and Emily to take me home, because I'm too tired to deal with any more judgy classmates and sleazeball guys. Hopefully, someone else will do something stupid soon and the rumor mills will have a new target to focus on.

I drop my backpack on my desk and flop onto my bed. A piece of bright yellow paper flutters to the floor.

"Open Auditions for *The Music Man*: Monday, May 16, 5-8pm." Across the top of the page, in Mom's loopy handwriting, "I thought you might be interested in this. You have one week to show me that you're responsible enough to audition."

I bet I'd make a phenomenal Marian the Librarian.

Grabbing my notebook with one hand, I open my math text with the other, softly humming "Being in Love" as I begin working through the problems. Marian totally knew what she wanted, and she didn't sit back, waiting for it to happen. She didn't let her reputation or the stupid, gossipy people in town define who she was. She held her head high and ignored them all. And that's precisely what I'm going to do, in real life and on stage.

Maybe I'll even get Dave to try out for Professor Harold Hill, instead of hiding on the stage crew again. He could totally pull off that whole slick, con-man role.

And I wouldn't mind letting him fall in love with me.

Two days after I rock the *Music Man* auditions, Shane's waiting on the front porch when I get home from school, rocking slowly back and forth in the porch swing with a large, brightly wrapped package in his lap.

"Laina's not home yet," I say. "She's still up at the lake with Rachel and Marsa."

Today was Laina's eighteenth birthday and Senior Ditch Day, all rolled into one. To celebrate, Miss Perfect decided to toss her perfect attendance record and spend some time with her friends.

Her real friends.

Kendra tried to guilt-trip her out of it. Her dad doesn't believe in Senior Ditch Day, and he threatened to drop by the school at random times to make sure she didn't skip with the rest of the seniors. Kendra said she'd never forgive Laina if she had to spend the whole day at school all by herself, but for once, my sister stood her ground. She slept over at Marsa's house last night with all of her old friends, and this morning, they went fishing up at Crystal Lake.

Laina didn't even bother to beg for Kendra's forgiveness. I've never been so proud of her in my life.

"Yeah, I know," Shane says. "I wanted to talk to you before she gets home."

I sit on the swing beside him, careful to keep a wide space between us. The last time a boy came to me for advice about my sister, it didn't end well.

"Well?" I ask, when he doesn't say anything. "What's up?"

"Laina's avoiding me again." He shifts the box in his lap and twirls the ends of the curly ribbon around his fingertips. "I thought we were making progress since she got in that fight with Kendra. She let me eat lunch with her yesterday." He looks at me and shrugs. "I even managed to talk to her without sounding like a drunken frat boy."

"So? It doesn't sound like she's avoiding you. You did know that today's Ditch Day, right? You had to notice the senior classes were practically empty."

He shakes his head and studies the package in his lap. "No, I knew she was going to the lake. Rachel said she'd talk to her for me." He stares at the fluffy clouds floating by. "But we kind of had plans last night. Adam and I were supposed to come see them at Marsa's house, but when we showed up, no one was home."

"Maybe they ran out for snacks. It doesn't mean she was avoiding you."

"We waited for over two hours. They never came back."

"Well, I'm glad to hear you weren't acting like some psycho stalker boy." I roll my eyes. "My advice? Don't mention it when she comes home."

"But how will I know if she even wants me here?"

"If she doesn't kick you off the porch, you're probably good." I point to the package on his lap. "I assume you're waiting to wish her a happy birthday?"

"Yeah. I figured nothing else has worked. I might as well try making a fool of myself one last time." He looks at me and pulls another, smaller, package out of his pocket. "I have a backup gift. A bracelet. In case you tell me this one is stupid."

"So what's in the big box?"

He blushes. "Okay, it's really dumb, but I was thinking about how you said I should do something big. And obviously, my prom plans blew up in my face." He leans back and stares at the sky. "I put together some things that made me think of her. A bag of Hershey Kisses. The dark chocolate kind, because I know that's her favorite. A toy car. An I.O.U. for a trip to Disneyland. And a CD with a bunch of songs that make me think of her. Including her song."

He groans and hides the package under the swing. "It's stupid, isn't it? I should just give her the bracelet."

"No. Jewelry is too much. You're not even together yet, and the big box is perfect. When she opens it, you can tell her how you feel. But do yourself a favor this time. Just say it. My sister's not very big on taking hints."

As if on cue, Laina's car pulls up in front of the house and she steps out, looking completely exhausted, but happier than I've seen her in months.

"I'll let you guys talk," I say. "But don't you dare make her cry." I wave at Laina and slip into the house before she reaches the porch.

Mom's on the phone, grinning like crazy and practically dancing around the kitchen, pulling things out of the cupboards. "Oh," she says into the phone. "Andi just walked in. I'll fill her in on the details and have her call you back."

She hangs up and smiles at me. "Jarod wants to

surprise Laina with a birthday picnic tonight. I have to go convince your father that it's okay for her to miss curfew, so I told Jarod you'd help him get everything ready." She glances out the window, to where Laina and Shane are talking on the porch. "Make sure she's still here when he comes by to pick her up. And it might be a good idea to get rid of that boy. Oh, and could you finish packing the basket for me? Everything's on the counter."

She dances out of the room without waiting for my response.

An old picnic basket, a bottle of sparkling grape juice and two fancy crystal glasses, chocolate-covered strawberries, and a small, double fudge chocolate cake are piled together on the counter. I hope Jarod has the rest of the picnic, because Laina will freak if he tries to feed her nothing but junk food.

I slowly pack everything into the basket while watching Shane and Laina through the window. I know Mom wants Jarod to win, but Laina's been in love with Shane for years. If he's finally going to do something about it, I should give him a chance.

Mom skips back into the kitchen. "Is everything ready?" She looks out the window and frowns. "Jarod will be here in an hour, and I'm afraid this conversation isn't winding down fast enough. Why don't you see what you can do about that while I take this basket over to the Johnson's house?"

I watch Laina and Shane, sitting on the porch steps, smiling and laughing. I haven't seen my sister so relaxed in a long time. Maybe I should let Shane hang out here until Jarod arrives. One big, final confrontation, where Laina can finally decide between them.

She deserves to choose her own happiness.

But then Shane says something, and Laina's smile turns into a frown. He stands up and kicks a loose rock, sending it skittering down the sidewalk. Angry voices fill the air, and then everything goes silent. Laina moves to the porch swing, tears in her eyes, and Shane follows her. He reaches for her hand, and when she pulls away, he sits beside her, staring at his feet. I don't know what he said, but he promised he wouldn't hurt her again, and he broke that promise.

She needs someone who won't ever make her cry.

I grab the phone and run to the door. "Laina, Jarod's on the phone. He says he wants you. Oops! I mean, he wants to talk to you." I blush and giggle, then duck back inside, as if I'm embarrassed by my mistake.

Through the window, I see Laina jump up and run after me. Halfway across the porch, she hesitates and turns back to say something to Shane. He shakes his head and storms away.

So I guess it's official. Laina chose Jarod.

I flop into a chair and put the phone to my ear, giggling into dead air as Laina storms into the house. I giggle and laugh, holding up a finger to signal for her to wait, until she finally gets frustrated and stomps down the hall to her bedroom. Then, I shakily dial Jarod's number to let him know she'll be here, waiting for his surprise.

Step Twelve: Having had a spiritual awakening, or some such nonsense, as a result of this process, we resolve to carry our message to all second-class siblings. Or at least to the perfect older sisters who aren't yet convinced of who they are.

Chapter Thirty-Three

Jarod finally beat up Anthony Matthews.

Anthony was bugging Laina again before school this morning, and Jarod ambushed him on the south stairs after second period. Anthony went home with a broken nose, a cracked rib, and a mild concussion. Jarod went home with a three-day suspension.

When Emily tells me about the fight at lunchtime, I expect that old, jealous twinge to knot up my stomach again, but I've got nothing. The only pang in my tummy is hunger. And that's easily solved with a mountain of chili-cheese fries and a carton of chocolate milk.

Emily looks across the cafeteria to the empty seat at Jarod's usual table. "Rachel said Jarod didn't even say a word. He jumped on poor Anthony and started pounding him for no reason."

"That's not what I heard," Summer says. "Josh told me that Marsa told him that Jarod said something like 'I'll kill you if you ever say another word to Alaina.' So what's that all about?" She turns to me with wide eyes, waiting for an explanation.

I shrug and shove a forkful of chili fries in my mouth. Anthony totally deserved every bruise and broken bone. But I'm not about to feed the gossip.

Dave reaches around me and snags one of my fries, popping it into his mouth before I can take it back. "Maybe Jarod got tired of quietly lusting after Alaina from afar and decided to finally do something about it."

I pull my tray away and shoot him a dirty look. "Eat your own lunch. I'm hungry."

He grins and takes a swig from my half-empty carton of milk. "Gotta keep my strength up. You wouldn't want me to faint on the way to the theater to see how our auditions went, would you?"

"Whatever. I'm a growing girl, and you're not being much of a gentleman." I grab one of his chicken nuggets and pop it into my mouth. And I promptly spit it into my napkin. "Oh, my gazebo, that's disgusting."

"Is there something going on between your sister and Anthony?" Emily asks. "Because I don't blame her. He's kind of hot."

"He's what?" Pete asks, pulling away from her with a frown.

"Not that he could compare to you, sweetie." Emily pats Pete's cheek and kisses him. Then, she turns her attention back to me.

"Laina and Anthony? Not a chance," I say. "They used to be friends, I think, way back when, but not anymore." I let my voice trail off. I can't really explain without saying too much. "Don't you think he's kind of an arrogant jerk?" I glance across the cafeteria to Laina's table. Her seat is also empty, and the Witch is desperately trying, and failing miserably, to take Laina's place as the center of attention.

Em shrugs. "I don't really know him."

"I bet I know why Jarod flipped out," Summer says, leaning across the table in full-on gossip mode. "This morning, Anthony was being a total creeper in the commons area before school. He thought he was being funny, but he so wasn't." She pauses and waits for us to lean forward expectantly. "Anthony announced that he was gonna sleep with Alaina, and when she said no, he picked her up and started to carry her out to the parking lot."

She rolls her eyes. "It's not like he actually would've done anything, because, duh, he's not stupid enough to think he can get away with rape with a room full of witnesses. But Alaina was pretty freaked out. She was all shaking and screaming, like she really thought he was gonna try something right here at school."

Emily shakes her head and sits back. "Sometimes, I think Alaina's a little too Snow White innocent. Everything's such high drama with her. She can't even take a joke."

I push my tray over to Dave. I've totally lost my appetite.

"And how many people in that room full of witnesses actually lifted a finger to stop Anthony before Jarod showed up?" I ask. "Did any of you do anything?"

Summer blushes slightly and won't meet my eyes. "Well, no," she says, "but he was playing around. He couldn't actually do anything without getting caught."

I slam my fist on the table. "You all saw what was happening, and you all thought it was some huge, hilarious act. No one even said a word." I push away from the table and stand up. "What if Jarod hadn't stopped him? What if Anthony got her alone? What if he came after her again later, when no one was around? Why would she even say anything, if she knew no one would listen?"

I stomp out of the cafeteria. It's no wonder Laina freaks out. And I don't blame Jarod for being so overprotective. He's the only one in this entire school she can count on.

I hide in a locked bathroom stall until the bell rings. Then, I dry my eyes and splash cold water on my face to get rid of the puffiness. I wish I could cry prettily like Laina does, but even after washing my face, I still look like I've been crying.

I can't go to class.

I walk straight to Ms. Detweiler's office and tell her the whole story, including my snooping in Laina's diary, what I learned from Jarod, and the "hilarious" conversation I suffered through at lunch. When I'm done telling her all about how she's lost control of her school, I pick up the phone and call my mom.

I'm not even lying when I tell her that I'm sick.

Dave stands on the front porch with a bunch of slightly-wilted daisies in one hand, and a thick stack of papers in the other. "Hey, Marian. Mrs. Mason let me grab your script for you. I hope you don't mind that I dropped by without calling." He holds out the papers, but before I can take them, he changes his mind and offers me the flowers instead. A half second later, he changes his mind again. He laughs nervously, wraps the script around the bouquet, and shoves it toward me with both hands. "These are for you."

"Thanks." I take the script-wrapped bouquet and hug it to my chest.

"Do you want to talk?" Dave shuffles his feet nervously. "You were really upset at lunch."

I shake my head and glance over my shoulder into the house. Laina got home from school an hour ago, and she's acting like the thing that happened with Anthony this morning was totally not a big deal. She's all mad at Jarod, insisting he shouldn't have punched Anthony, because she can be friends with anyone she wants. And she threw a huge temper tantrum when she found out that I told Ms. Detweiler about her diary. She'd never forgive me if she caught me talking about it with Dave, too.

I'm pretty sure Laina blames herself for what happened this morning. And I don't know how to convince her that it's not her fault.

I step out onto the porch and close the door. "I can't really talk about it." I glance back at the house. I walk over to the porch swing and sit, watching a meadowlark darting back and forth, carrying something to the nest in the roof.

Dave nods and crosses over to sit beside me. "Is this about Jarod? Because, you know, that doesn't really mean anything. He was sticking up for his best friend." He squeezes my hand quickly, and then he lets go and pulls away. "I would've jumped Anthony too, if I'd known. It doesn't mean he chose her."

I shake my head. "I'm not jealous." I want to tell him everything, but it's not my story to tell. "I have a plan. Will you help me?"

Dave nods slowly. "Andi, you know I'd do anything you ask." He frowns. "I guess everyone's a chump for someone, huh?"

Laina paces back and forth across her bedroom, wild eyes flashing. "It's not fair. Nick invited everyone in our class. Every. Single. Person."

I grab her shoulders and force her to look at me.

"You're going to give yourself a stroke if you don't calm down. Trust me. You're not missing a thing. I'm not going to Nick's party either."

She collapses onto her bed and hugs Mr. Cuddles. "At least you had a choice. Do you know how embarrassing it was when he tracked me down to make sure I knew he doesn't want me there?" She sighs. "The last party of my high school career, and Nick invited everyone but me. He invited the biggest nerd in school, and I'm still not cool enough. The one time I decide to actually have some fun, and I'm officially uninvited."

I laugh. "And you say I'm a drama queen? Please. You know you'd hate it. He doesn't want you to be uncomfortable." Nick totally agreed when I said his parties aren't the place for someone as Snow White innocent as Laina. And we practiced what he would say, so I know he was really cool about it when he talked to her.

She buries her face in Mr. Cuddles' tummy and sobs. I shake my head and bite my lip so she won't see me smiling. She's totally going to thank me later.

"You know what we should do?" I squeal, pulling the teddy bear out of her arms. "We should go miniature golfing, like when we were little. Won't that be crazy fun?"

She stares at me, like I've grown another head. Because Laina always hated putt-putt golf. She only pretended to like it because it used to be my favorite.

"Oh, come on," I say. "I'll even allow creative putting."

Laina shakes her head. "I don't know. I don't really feel like playing a game where I have to cheat so I don't suck." But she gets out of bed, which means I've already convinced her.

"Yay!" I grab black skinny jeans and a tank top out of her closet and toss her an emerald green cardigan, the same color as Jarod's eyes. "Put these on." I dig through the bottom of the closet until I unearth the black, strappy sandals I bought for her birthday last week. "And wear these. They're perfect."

"But those hurt my feet," Laina says. "You know I don't like heels."

I sigh. "Beauty isn't about comfort, and everyone knows Barbie is supposed to wear heels. These are totally sexy. So you're wearing them. Now, what accessories will work with that?"

I turn to raid her jewelry box, but I stop mid-turn when I see the locket around her neck. The one Jarod bought for her birthday. She grabs the locket and holds it tightly. "What's wrong with this?"

I bite my lip and take a deep breath. I'm definitely doing the right thing. "It's perfect." I flash a carefree smile. "Now get dressed. I have to make a quick call, and then I'll be right back to do your hair and makeup."

It's time for Cinderella to get her prince, and I'm the perfect fairy godmother to make it happen.

I call Dave to let him know everything's going according to plan, and then I tell Jarod to meet Laina at the Putt-A-Round Mini Golf behind the mall. By the time I throw on some clothes and run a brush through my hair, Laina's waiting for me.

My hands are shaking like crazy, and it takes more than half an hour to do her makeup and pin her hair back away from her face. By the time I finish, Dave's already waiting by the front door, wearing a dark, fitted suit and the ridiculous chauffer's cap I borrowed from the costume closet of the Little Community Theater.

He looks totally hot.

"Your chariot awaits, ladies," he says with a bow.

Laina pulls me into the bathroom. "I can't crash your date, just because I'm a social leper. Dave's been trying to get you to go out with him since he broke up with Heather, and I'm not going to ruin things." She smiles. "You go. I'll say I have a headache or something."

"No way. I'm not letting you back out that easily.

Remember how much fun the three of us had that one night? When he was following us all over town? Well, this might be the last time we get to go hang out like this before you go off to college and abandon me." I bat my eyes at her and put on my best puppy dog pout.

"We have all summer to do things. It's not like I'm leaving tomorrow."

"But it's not the same. And this tricycle needs a third wheel, so don't you dare back out on me now."

She laughs, and I drag her out of the bathroom before she tries to back out again. We drive to the Putt-A-Round, and Dave plays his role perfectly, totally sidetracking Laina every time she tries to ask about the details for our plan tonight.

As soon as we get inside the arcade attached to the mini golf course, I put phase two in motion. "Wow, it's really crowded tonight," I say, looking around at all the screaming kids and frowning slightly.

Laina shakes her head. Before she can argue that we should've listened when she suggested going out to dinner instead, I grab Dave's hand. "You wait here." I push Laina onto an empty bench along one wall. "We'll go check on the wait time for mini golf." I pull Dave through the crowd of kids until I know she can't see us anymore, and then we backtrack to the door and out into the parking lot.

She won't follow us, because she's already feeling guilty about crashing our date. And by the time she realizes we've left, Jarod should be here. He promised he wouldn't blow it, but in case she feels like running, those strappy sandals I forced her to wear should make sure she doesn't get very far.

Dave drives to the park and pulls up to the lake. "I know there's no footbridge," he says, "but I thought we could run lines and practice our big scene." He takes my hand and walks to a secluded bench near the water.

I sit down, a smile playing across my lips as I watch the

ripples blowing softly across the water in the breeze. "What big scene would that be, Dave?"

"That's Professor Harold Hill to you, Marion." He grins and slides close to me, wrapping his arms around my waist. "And we should rehearse the scene where you meet me at the bridge to tell me that you love me."

"Oh no. I think we need more practice with the bit in the library. When I'm totally not fooled by your charm. That's probably the most critical scene."

He cups my cheek in his hand and brushes his thumb across my lips, totally ignoring my nervous outburst. "And then I'll admit that I love you too, Marian the Librarian."

He kisses me softly, winding his fingers through my hair as he pulls me into him. My breath catches and my heart thumps as the kiss deepens, and then suddenly, he's pulling away.

"Wait a minute." He pulls a piece of paper out of his pocket. "That's not quite right. You missed your line. Aren't you supposed to say you love me, too? I'm sure it's in the script."

Dave's wrong. Professor Harold Hill and Marian the Librarian don't even say the words "I love you" in the foot bridge scene.

I take the page from him and toss it aside before melting into his arms. "I think we should write our own script. And keep practicing until we get it right."

Acknowledgments

This book wouldn't exist without the help of some very important people, who inspired and encouraged me every step along the way.

First, I would like to thank the two people without whom this story never would have been told: Shawn Curtis, thank you for helping me to find my voice, providing inspiration for one of my favorite characters (two, actually), and walking me through the creation of Alaina Andersen's story. (And for all of the Facebook chats whenever I was stuck on a scene!)

And an extra special Thank You to my little sister, Angie Murphy, for insisting that Laina's little sister, Andi, needed a chance to tell *her* side of the story. Without the page of "fan fiction" you wrote, I never would have seen Andi's story.

I could never have written any of this without the love and support of my amazing family. Thank you for everything you do for me! Phil, my Prince Charming, who still makes my heart flutter after eighteen years. Benjamin, my favorite (only) son, and the best cheerleader I could ask for. Emily, who helped me write Andi's twelve-step program during an especially cold wait in a very long line. Rebekah, who did lots of cartwheels to celebrate my book deal, since I didn't have the balance to do it for myself. And Katherine, who carefully read the entire draft to find redundancies and typos.

Giant squish hugs and thanks to my amazing critique partners who helped shape Andi's world. Ashley Turcotte, who read more drafts than I can count and held my hand through countless self-doubt moments. Brenda Drake, who kept me sane and gave me the push I needed to actually send my story out into the world. Without you, my story would still be sitting in the hard drive of my computer. Rachel Solomon, who read an early draft and helped me pinpoint all of the little plot holes I'd forgotten to fill. And my awesome Maryland critique group: Laura Shovan, Amie Rose Rotruck, Jackie Douge, Marjory Bancroft, Connie Morgan and Barbara Dell. I am a stronger writer because of you all.

    Thank you to my mom, who always encouraged me to keep writing, and who answered my frantic calls when I had questions on proper punctuation and grammar issues. My dad, who never takes anything seriously, and who would have played right along with Nick's prom night teasing. And my siblings, Carin, Angie, Sheryl, Robert, Steven, John, and Mark, who taught me that siblings can love each other like crazy, even when they're driving each other insane. And thank you to my "adopted" sister, Susie, for sending me story pencils from all over the world. One quarter of the words for this book came pouring out of your pencils.

    I'm so grateful for all of the amazing writers who have encouraged and supported me along the way. Jason Wright, thank you for setting the spark in motion and giving me the push to sharpen my very first story pencil. And thank you for taking the time out of your busy schedule to have lunch with me and give me pointers when I was starting out. Laura Bowers and Lois Szymanski, thank you for your insightful critiques, and for encouraging me to swallow my fears and let my story make its way out into the world. Summer Heacock, Sharon Johnston and Literary Cupid, thank you for picking me for your teams in the online pitch contests that introduced TWELVE STEPS to the world, and for your continued support and encouragement. Rachel Harris, you are my hero. I am truly blessed to call you my friend. Thank you for always being there for me, when I have a question or when I just need someone to squeal with when I have news that I'm not yet ready to share with everyone.

Love and gratitude to the best agent ever, Jessica Sinsheimer. Thank you for answering all of my questions and helping me through all of the behind-the-scenes stuff that goes into making a book happen. And for reminding me that this race is a marathon, not a sprint.

Thank you a million times over to Mandy Schoen, my amazing editor. I couldn't have asked for a better person to work with on my debut novel. Your love for Andi and her story kept me going through all of the tough revisions, and I can honestly say that I love this book more now than I did when this whole process began. Thank you for pushing me to dig deeper. I couldn't have done it without you!

And last, but certainly not least, a giant thank you to my friends and followers on Twitter, who remind me daily why I write. To my nieces and nephews, who let me use their names for the supporting characters in this story. To the Cheyenne East High School class of '95, who inspired many of Andi's adventures.

Especially that one boy who became Nick Carver. I never got the courage to tell you that I had a giant crush on you in high school, but you still managed to turn my ragged self-esteem into an ego made of awesome.

Thank you.

About the Author

Veronica Bartles grew up in Wyoming and currently lives in Maryland with her husband and four children. As the second of eight children and the mother of four, Veronica Bartles is no stranger to the ups and downs of sibling relationships. She uses this insight to write stories about siblings who mostly love each other, even while they're driving one another crazy. When Veronica's not writing or lost in the pages of her newest favorite book, she enjoys creating delicious desserts, exploring new places, and knitting with recycled materials.

TWELVE STEPS is Veronica's first novel. Her debut picture book, THE PRINCESS AND THE FROGS, is coming November 15, 2016 from Balzer & Bray / Harper Collins.

Connect with Veronica online:
- Website: **http://vbartles.com**
- Facebook: **http://facebook.com/AuthorVeronicaBartles**
- Twitter: @vbartles
- VBartles Design: **http://vbartles.com/design.htm**

Made in the USA
Middletown, DE
22 December 2018